Making Tracks
British Carrier Story 1914 to 1972

by Peter Chamberlain and Chris Ellis

AFV/Weapons Series Editor Duncan Crow

Profile Publications Limited Windsor Berkshire England

Other Profile Books

Other Famous Profile Bound Volume Series

© Profile Publications Limited 1973
ISBN 0 85383 0886
First published in 1973 by
Profile Publications Limited
Windsor Berkshire England

Printed in England by Edwin Snell printers, Yeovil, Somerset

Contents

About the Authors

Peter Chamberlain is internationally famous as an author of books and articles on AFVs. He first became interested in tanks during his World War II service in the Royal Engineers when his unit in the Western Desert was responsible for the rendering safe of captured enemy weapons and explosives. A natural off-shoot of this critical work was his first-hand familiarisation with German and Italian tanks and other equipment. After the war he began his collection of photographs, documents, and books which has made him one of the leading repositories of World War II military information. For many years he has been associated with the Imperial War Museum in the enormous task of identifying, captioning and indexing the plethora of wartime photographs that accrue to it. He is the co-author of more than a dozen *Profiles* in the AFV/Weapons Series.

Chris Ellis is an accomplished writer in the fields of military history and model-making. Formerly editor of *Airfix Magazine* he is currently editor of *Modelworld*. He has been co-author with Peter Chamberlain of many authoritative publications on AFVs, including nine *Profiles* in the AFV/Weapons Series.

Acknowledgments

For assistance with the enormous task of compiling photographs and information for this book the authors would like to thank The Imperial War Museum (both Photographic and Reference Libraries), in particular D. Mayne, G. Pavey, and D. Nash of these departments. Thanks are also due to Colonel Robert J. Icks (US Army Rtd.), R. P. Hunnicutt, John F. Milsom, B. H. Vanderveen, M. P. Conniford, R. Surlemont, and Alvis Ltd. for valuable assistance.

Line up of the Motor Machine Gun Brigade in June 1918 for inspection by General Horne.

British Infantry Carriers 1914-1972

by Peter Chamberlain and Chris Ellis

INTRODUCTION

THOUGH tanks and tank battles capture most of the popular imagination and the tank is commonly thought of as the main battlefield weapon of today, it is not untrue to say that what became the tank as we know it is merely a by-product of an earlier quest for battlefield mobility. The tank as an armoured fighting vehicle in its own right happened to evolve from ideas which in the first place were concerned with ways of moving infantrymen about on a battlefield with the maximum immunity from the enemy. Various individuals in different countries realised the military potential of mechanised vehicles almost as soon as this mode of transport became a proven practical proposition in the 1890s and early 1900s. Davidson in America, Simms in Britain, and Genty in France were just three of the most prominent pioneers who showed that light road vehicles could be utilised to carry a machine gun and its crew over vast distances well beyond the capabilities of marching infantrymen; they also showed that these vehicles could be used for patrol work much more efficiently than cavalry. From these

beginnings came the development of armoured cars on the one hand and the use of trucks (or even buses) to carry infantry sections on the other.

All this was well before 1914. The Great War created the conditions which led to the fusing of the two developments into the armoured personnel (or infantry) carrier, though the gestation period was surprisingly protracted. From the early days of the fighting the machine gun dominated the battlefield more effectively than had been foreseen by the generals. The Germans in particular excelled at the art because they had more machine guns. Thousands of Allied troops died trying to take a few yards of ground and the front line became a stalemate of opposing trench systems. In such conditions as these inventive French and British minds began to devise ways of moving infantry and their machine guns forward to take German trenches behind a moving protective armoured shield. The "shield", typically, took the form of an armoured tractor with the men crouching inside. The original "landship" ideas of two British tank pioneers, Swinton and Sueter, were vehicles of this type.

However, the development of the "landship" took a

1

1 *Early type of motorised machine gun carrier, The Simms quadricycle of 1899.*

2 *Another type of early motorised machine gun carrier was the AC tricar, built by Auto-Carriers Ltd. A number of these vehicles with special bodies to carry either a Vickers MG or ammunition were supplied to the Army in 1910 and were used by the 25th Cyclist Battalion (A City of London Territorial Unit) during manoeuvres.*

3 *The Battle of Amiens in August 1918 was one of the first occasions when British infantry were carried forward in armoured vehicles in support of a tank attack. The lengthened tank, Mk V* was used for this role.*

4 *The idea of the motor-cycle machine gun combination persisted in the British Army until 1940–41. These equipments were used in recce regiments but their vulnerability in the face of air and tank attack led to their abandonment. The weapons carried by these vehicles varied, and included the Vickers MG, Bren LMG or Boys anti-tank rifle.*

5 *The Vickers Clyno motor-cycle was the most successful early motor machine gun equipment. Though not strictly an infantry carrier, its role was the same as that later taken over by carriers. The machine gun could be mounted to face in either direction or dismounted to be used in a ground role.*

6 *Motor-cycle combination with Boys anti-tank gun.*

7 *Mechanised infantry in the British Army for much of World War II still depended on the 15 cwt truck for mobility, even in some armoured divisions. Later in the war, half-track and Kangaroo vehicles became available. The picture shows men of the Northumberland Fusiliers, a machine gun battalion in 1941.*

slight turn in another direction during its short evolutionary period in 1915–16, and what started as an "armoured caterpillar" for carrying troops became a landship proper with large calibre guns and a specialist crew whose main task was to neutralise enemy machine gun teams and put the infantry to rout. This set the pattern for a future line of tank development—in the form of the "infantry tank"—up to 1940 and beyond. The infantry remained unarmoured and followed up the tank on foot.

The first British armoured infantry carriers in tracked form were not developed until 1918. They evolved partly from the use of supply tanks in 1917. These were disarmed "war weary" vehicles used to carry up stores and ammunition in support of the fighting tanks during a tank advance. Infantry were sometimes carried forward on or in the supply tanks to consolidate captured ground. Early British tank tacticians, notably Swinton and Fuller, were strong advocates of specialist troop carriers, especially for use in the major tank attacks which were envisaged in huge frontal assaults for the planned 1919 campaigns. In 1918 a standard Mk V tank was modified to make a troop carrier by having its sponsons removed and replaced by sliding shutter-type doors from which infantrymen could disembark either side of the vehicle. Subsequently a specialist supply and troop carrier tank, the Mk IX, was built in limited numbers. This had side doors and a large internal capacity, though its development was prematurely terminated at the end of the war. On the Western Front, meanwhile, the standard Mk V tank was lengthened with extra hull sections to make the Mk V* (and a Mk V** version was purpose-built to a similar design). These lengthened tanks were intended to carry a few infantrymen and some were first used in this armoured troop carrier role at the Battle of Amiens in August 1918. Experience here pointed up the limitations of the idea, for the fumes from the exposed engines and the violent motion of the unsprung vehicle meant that the troops disembarked sick and dizzy, not to say disoriented, at the very time they needed to be in trim fighting form.

The Armistice of November 1918 brought official ideas of armoured troop carriers to a halt. It is interesting to note, however, that for other infantry roles wheeled armoured troop carriers pre-dated the tanks. In 1914 a go-ahead French-Canadian patriot persuaded some rich industrialists to finance some Autocar trucks and give them armoured bodies. These were actually the first

Commonwealth armoured vehicles built for their intended role. In 1915, also, a unit of the British Army in India had a commercial truck armoured, complete with rifle ports, for use in patrolling riot areas at a time of civil disturbance. This idea was revived for the British security forces in Ireland at the time of the Irish Troubles, 1919–1922. Here various types of trucks were given armoured bodies for street patrol work. (In this respect history could repeat itself for in 1970 in Northern Ireland British infantry units were using armoured trucks for the same purpose).

In the peacetime years, however, such development that took place with infantry carriers was restricted almost solely to the light tracked carriers which emanated from the "tankette" ideas of the 1920s. These in turn stemmed largely from the severe restrictions on defence spending at the time. Once again Tank Corps advocates of infantry support in armoured attacks were largely behind the original tankette idea which was to provide cheap tracked vehicles in which individual infantrymen could move about a battlefield. This led to the developments of light tanks proper (beyond the scope of this book) and the infantry carrier which was mainly seen as a means of moving machine gun teams and reconnaissance personnel around the battlefield. The development of the many light carriers involved forms the bulk of this book. Germany, with more money to spend adopted the purpose-built half-track carrier for motorised armoured infantry, with spectacular results in the 1940–41 period and afterwards. The principles had been advocated and demonstrated by British tank tacticians in the 1920s and 1930s though the British themselves, for both political and financial reasons never developed this form of vehicle. Meanwhile both the French and the Americans emulated the German half-track idea to a certain extent.

During World War II, the British infantry was for the most part transported by lorry for the carrier in its various forms was not suitable for transporting more than two or three men so was restricted still largely to support and command roles. With the development of powerful armoured divisions for the 1944–45 campaigns the APC finally made its overdue appearance *en masse* in the British Army. Even so the arrangements were very extemporary—either American half-tracks supplied on Lease-Lend (and never available in sufficient quantities) or Kangaroos, which were redundant tanks with turrets removed and adapted to seat infantrymen. These vehicles performed a useful role, specially in NW Europe in 1944–45, but they were open-topped and in case of air attacks on ground targets this was less than satisfactory. The lessons of World War II were taken to heart, however, and in the quarter century which followed the British Army were first supplied with a family of wheeled APCs, then a family of tracked APCs which were similar to contemporary foreign designs.

This book sets out to record all British armoured infantry carriers and their variants in a handy reference form, as nearly as possible in chronological order. It presents more pictures of carrier types than have hitherto been presented in a single volume, and also includes a few associated types of vehicle, such as motor-cycle machine gun carriers which were not strictly armoured types but were all part of the same armoured infantry doctrine. Tactics as such are beyond the scope of this book but some indication of a vehicle's role and employment, as well as period of service, is given in the text.

Autocar Armoured Truck.

Armoured Lorry, RNAS.

Cadillac Armoured Car.

PART ONE

CARRIERS OF WORLD WAR I

Armoured Lorry, RNAS

One of the very earliest of all armoured personnel carriers to be used in war was the brainchild of the imaginative Commander C. R. Samson of the Royal Naval Air Service (RNAS). As is well known, the RNAS pioneered the use of armoured vehicles in the Great War. Commander Samson, one of the first naval aviators, was in charge of the RNAS air squadron sent to Dunkirk for anti-Zeppelin defence early in September 1914. To defend its airfields from attack by the Germans, Samson had armour plate fitted to a number of assorted cars, all subsequently adapted to carry machine guns. The value of mobility was thus appreciated at an early stage of the war by the RNAS, whose personnel later played the dominant part in developing British tanks. The cars were used for patrol, reconnaissance, and even raiding. It was soon realised that infantry could also be carried in armoured vehicles following up behind the armoured cars on raids and patrols, and Samson and his brother, a fellow officer, acquired two of the ex-London LGOC "B" Type buses which had been sent to France as troop transports. The bodies were removed and replaced with box-like bodies and covered cabs made from boiler plate

by a local engineering works (Forges et Chantiers) at Dunkirk. Loopholes for rifle fire were provided and 12 Royal Marines could be carried. The boiler plate gave immunity from rifle calibre bullets at about a quarter-mile. The design was quite effective and anticipated future vehicles of this type by several years. However, such was the effect on performance from the added weight of the plating, that the lorries could not keep up with the armoured cars. Hence in practice the lorries were not used and the marines were carried instead in modified touring cars. The armoured lorries were little used in their intended role.

Autocar Armoured Truck

The most advanced thinking in armoured carriers in 1914 emanated from Canada. Early in the Great War it was fashionable for individuals or bodies in Britain and the Commonwealth to sponsor and pay for individual items of equipment to assist the war effort. Several armoured car units were raised in Britain in this way. In Canada a French-Canadian called Raymond Brutinel, late of the French Army, was a great advocate of the importance of the machine gun. With the sponsorship of leading Canadian industrialists, Brutinel organised a force of twenty motor machine gun carriers which were basically Autocar commercial trucks with $\frac{3}{4}$ inch armour plate bodies made by Bethlehem Steel Co. The vehicles had open topped bodies with dropsides and an enclosed cab. Two Colt (later Vickers) machine guns and their crews were carried in each vehicle and the guns were fired either from the vehicle or from ground mounts in the conventional way. The unit formed part of 1st Canadian Motor Machine Gun Brigade which had the distinction of being the very first organised armoured unit with purpose-built vehicles. The brigade went to France in 1915 and served there for the rest of the Great War. It was another 20 years or so before armoured machine gun carriers really came into their own again with British or Commonwealth forces; Brutinel's thinking was well in advance of War Office ideas in the 1914–18 period.

Cadillac Armoured Car, Indian Pattern

One of the earliest of British armoured personnel carriers was a vehicle built in India on a commercial Cadillac car chassis. This was designed to carry infantry when quelling the frequent street riots and disorders prevalent in 1915 in Calcutta. A completely enclosed boiler plate body was built up of 5 mm sheets, with loopholes for rifle fire from within. The vehicle could carry two Maxim machine guns and up to six riflemen.

Fiat Armoured Car

Some armoured car units were formed for patrol work in NW India in 1915. These were not strictly speaking infantry units but they carried some infantrymen. Various requisitioned touring cars were given armoured (boiler plate) bodies and subsequently a few Fiat 30 cwt lorries were given armoured bodies by local railway workshops. These vehicles had open-topped bodies with a raised roof and there were loopholes for rifle or machine gun fire from within. One or two further vehicles were later built with fully enclosed armoured bodies and equipped as mobile workshops to maintain the mobile columns. These vehicles served in the 1915–1918 period.

Tank, Mk IX. Troop and Supply Carrier

The development of an armoured tracked vehicle, designed specifically for the carriage of troops was begun in September 1917. While this type of specialised vehicle was being designed by the Mechanical Warfare Depart-

ment, this function was performed by the adaptation of normal fighting tanks, in which the gun sponsons were replaced by mild steel boxes.

The first machine to be built as a troop or supply carrier was constructed by Messrs Armstrong-Whitworth in June 1918. Known as the Tank Mk IX, the basic design was similar to the standard tank then in use, but a maximum cargo space, 13 ft 6 in by 5 ft 5 in was achieved by moving the transmission gears to the rear of the vehicle and the engine forward; two large oval doors, either side of the Mk IX provided for easy access.

Able to carry 50 infantrymen or 10 tons of stores, 35 of the Mk IX series were built, none of which saw action due to the end of the war.

Brief details:
Crew 4
Weight 37 tons loaded   27 tons unladen
Length 31 ft 11 in
Width 8 ft 1 in
Height 7 ft 8 in
Max Armour 10 mm

During 1919, one Mk IX was modified for trials as an amphibious vehicle. Naval pontoons were attached to each side, a raised cab with extended exhausts was constructed on the front of the vehicle and hinged flaps or paddles attached at intervals on the tracks. Propulsion was by means of an auxiliary motor at the rear of the vehicle.

Fiat Armoured Car.

Tank, Mk IX. Troop and Supply Carrier.

Tank, Mk IX modified.

The Studebaker Tank.

The Studebaker Tank

This vehicle was ordered separately by the British War Mission in New York outside the auspices of the Tank Supply Department in Britain. Intended as a supply and troop carrier, only one prototype was built to the British Mission's requirements, the suppliers being the Studebaker Pierce-Arrow Export Corp. With the 1918 Armistice the project was abandoned.

PART TWO
DRAGON GUN TRACTORS

Intimately related to the development of the tracked carrier was a specialised vehicle known as the "Dragon", a corruption of the term "drag gun". Dragons were developed as tracked gun tractors during the 1920s and these vehicles were able to carry a gun detachment, a supply of ammunition and tow a gun. It was from a later light type of dragon that the Vickers-Bren machine gun carrier was evolved.

The first standard dragon, the Mk I was issued to Field Brigades of the Field Artillery for towing the 18 pdr field gun. As these machines were found unsatisfactory they were replaced by the Dragon Mk II, a more powerful machine with improved suspension and better armour protection for the engine, driver and gun crew. The Mk III introduced in 1925 was an improved type Mk II, with revised gear ratios to enable this machine to tow medium artillery, the 60 pdr gun and 6 in howitzer; more accommodation was provided for the personnel. The designation of this vehicle was later changed to Dragon, Medium Mk III.

Dragon, Mk I towing 18 pdr field gun.

Dragon, Mk II towing 18 pdr field gun.

Above: *Dragon, Medium. Mk III towing 6 in Howitzer.*   Below: *Dragon, Medium. Mk III showing ammunition lockers.*

Dragon, Medium. Mk IIIA.

Dragon, Medium. Mk IIIB towing 6 in Howitzer.

Dragon, Medium. Mk IIIC.

Dragon, Mk II*.

The Dragon, Medium Mk IIIA introduced in 1926 was similar in performance to the Medium Mk III but embodied certain improvements found to be advantageous by experience with the Mk III. These included a new design of suspension with an extra return roller, side skirting with mud chutes and a ventilating louvre fitted in the left upper side plate to facilitate cooling of the engine compartment. There was also a modified front. During 1927 it was decided to convert the Mk II Dragon to haul medium artillery. Re-designated Mk II* the conversion chiefly consisted of strengthening the steering

clutches and reducing the final drive ratio to allow the vehicle to tow 60 pdr and 6 in artillery equipment. The ammunition lockers for the field gun were replaced by lockers for the medium equipments. The Medium Mk IIIB was introduced in 1928 to meet a further request for medium artillery tractors. This model was generally similar to the Mk IIIA but was fitted with suspension in which the six track return rollers were sprung in pairs, mounted on leaf springs. The headlights were housed in box containers, and the engine compartment was divided from the crew and driver's compartments by a heat protection screen that extended above the hull top. The last of this series of Dragons, based on a chassis that was similar to that of the Vickers Medium Tank, was the Dragon, Medium Mk IIIC, introduced in 1932. This again was similar to the Mk IIIB but with the cooling louvres in the left side plate omitted and with certain other modifications. The final type of the medium Dragons appeared in 1935, designated Dragon, Medium Mk IV. This machine was based on the running gear of the Vickers-Armstrong 6 ton tank and was fitted with a re-designed superstructure and an AEC diesel engine.

Dragon, Medium. Mk IV towing 60 pdr gun.

Dragon, Light. Mk I.

LIGHT DRAGONS

Circa 1928–1929 it was decided by the War Office to replace the heavy expensive Dragons as gun tractors for field artillery equipment (18 pdr) with a cheaper light type of tracked vehicle.

Various experimental vehicles were submitted for trials and the machine that was finally selected went into limited production during 1930. Designated Dragon, Light, Mark I, this open hull vehicle was equipped with the horizontal coil spring Horstmann suspension that was then in use with the Vickers Light Tank, Mk II.

Dragon, Light. Mk IA.

With modifications that included the re-arrangement of the crew seating and the raising of the vehicle sides a second version was produced that was known as the Light, Dragon Mk IA of which only a few were built.

During 1932, Dragons, Light, Mk II and IIA appeared. Though similar in appearance to the Mk IA, these vehicles were equipped with a number of modifications and improvements that included a side swivel canopy, and a modified suspension with two return track rollers,

Dragon, Light. Mk II towing 4.5 in Howitzer.

Dragon, Light. Mk IIB towing ammunition limbers.

Dragon, Light. Mk IIC towing 3.7 in Howitzer.

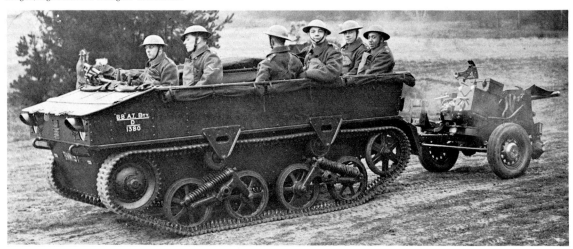

Dragon, Light. Mk IIC towing 2 pdr anti-tank gun.

as used on Light Tanks, Mk IIA and IIB. In 1933, with the planned increase in production of the Light Dragon, further improvements and modifications were made; these included an improved Horstmann suspension with inclined double springs, as fitted to Light Tank, Mk III, the fitting of triangular steel plates to support the spindles carrying the track return rollers, reinforcement of the vehicle side plates, moulded rubber rear track guards to prevent damage on fouling the limber, protective covering on the side exhaust pipe and improvement in the

cooling system. These modified versions were designated Dragons, Light, Mk IIB, IIC and IID.

During 1934, as a commercial project, Vickers-Armstrong Ltd built a vehicle that could be adapted for two roles, either as a machine gun carrier or as a tractor for towing a light field gun. This vehicle, factory designation, VA D50 was equipped with Horstmann sloping coil spring suspension with three road wheels, two return rollers and a solid driving sprocket and idler wheel. The driver and co-driver were enclosed in an

Vickers experimental gun tractor, VA D50.

Dragon, Light. Mk III prototype.

Universal Carrier, Mk I* towing 6 pdr anti-tank gun.

Dragon, Light. Mk III.

armoured compartment behind which were provided two folding benches on either side of the vehicle for seating the gun crew or an independent machine gun unit. (This vehicle with modifications was later tested as a self-propelled mount for a Vickers 40 mm gun and was designated, Tractor with 40 mm Equipment).

On February 1, 1935, a meeting was held at the War Office to discuss this new type of vehicle as a replacement for the complicated Light Dragons and Carden-Loyd Mk VI machine gun carrier then due to be replaced in service.

The War Office decided to purchase two modified versions of the VA D50 for trials, one as a Light Dragon and the other as a machine gun carrier; as the tests of these machines proved successful, both vehicles were put into production. Due to a change in policy however in favour of wheeled vehicles as gun tractors, the Dragon version of the new Vickers design, the Light Dragon Mk III was dropped after 69 vehicles had been built, but from the machine gun carrier version was begun a new line of development (See Part Five on The Machine Gun, Scout and Bren Carriers).

By 1939 many of the Light Dragons remaining in service were used for towing the 2 pdr anti-tank gun.

At this time the 2 pdr was still an artillery responsibility but, subsequently, it and its successor, the 6 pdr gun equipped infantry anti-tank companies. The Universal Carrier a direct descendant of the Light Dragon, the Loyd Carrier, the Windsor Carrier and the T16 Carrier were all used as towers for the 6 pdr anti-tank gun in later war years. Post-war, an enlarged derivative of the earlier types, the Oxford Carrier was developed (by which time the 17 pdr had become the infantry anti-tank gun) and trials of this vehicle as a gun tractor for the 17 pdr were carried out early in the post-war period. As a result of a shortage of Oxford Carriers, the Stuart Light Tank was adapted to tow the 17 pdr anti-tank gun. This consisted of the removal of the turret, re-arrangement of the vehicle's interior and the adding of the attachment for towing purposes. (A similar adaptation of tank to gun tractor was made during the war when the Crusader II chassis was given a new open superstructure and converted as a fast tractor for the 17 pdr anti-tank gun.)

By the time the FV 432 family of tracked carriers had appeared the infantry anti-tank gun had become recoilless portee equipment and the requirement for gun towers was dropped.

Loyd Carrier, Tracked Towing, No 1 Mk II towing 6 pdr anti-tank gun.

Oxford Carrier, towing 17 pdr anti-tank gun.

Windsor Carrier, towing 6 pdr anti-tank gun.

Universal Carrier, T16 towing 6 pdr anti-tank gun.

Crusader Gun Tractor, Mk I.

Universal Carrier, Mk III towing 120 mm recoilless anti-tank gun.

B

Stuart Gun Tractor towing 17 pdr anti-tank gun.

Martel prototype for One-Man Tankette.

Morris-Martel One-Man Tankette.

PART THREE
THE DEVELOPMENT OF THE MORRIS AND CARDEN-LOYD ONE AND TWO MAN TANKETTES

Morris-Martel Machines
The idea of armoured mobility for the infantryman had first been suggested in 1915 by the French General Estienne who envisaged the employment, in mass, of skirmishers mounted in armoured cross-country vehicles, thus replacing the foot soldier. This French project was later to emerge as the Renault FT, a light two-man tank.

After World War I, the idea of armoured mobile infantrymen was again revived by Colonel (later Major-General) J. F. C. Fuller, and several British Army Officers became interested. One of them, Major (later Lieutenant-General Sir Gifford) Le Q. Martel undertook during 1925 to construct a machine at his own expense. The vehicle was built in Major Martel's garage and was made entirely of ordinary commercial components, the engine being taken from an old Maxwell car and the back axle from a Ford lorry. The superstructure was made of wood. Only the tracks were specially made by the Roadless Traction Co. As a result of demonstrations given by Martel with his home-made

one-man machine, the War Office authorised the building of four modified factory-made machines, and the Morris Motor firm undertook to build them. Except for the tracks and armour they were constructed with Morris automotive parts with a 16 hp engine, the weight being just over two tons. The first machine was delivered in March 1926, followed by the other three, one of which was a two-man version. The one-man tank concept was later dropped as it was realised that one crewman could not control the machine and handle the machine gun at the same time. Eight modified machines of the two-man version were later ordered in 1927 to be employed as scout machines with the Experimental Mechanised Force then being formed. A novel feature of these vehicles was an adjustable driver's seat. which could be lowered six inches so as to bring the driver's head within the vehicle's superstructure when engaged in action.

Brief details:

Crew 2
Weight 2.75 tons
Length 9 ft 10 in
Width 4 ft 7 in
Height 5 ft 6 in
Engine 16 hp Morris 4-cylinder water cooled
Max speed 15 mph (road) 10 mph (cross country)

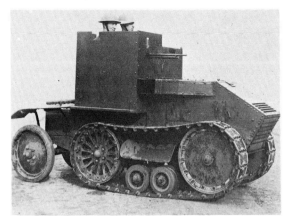

Morris-Martel Two-Man Tankette.

Crossley-Martel One-Man Tankette.

Crossley-Martel One-Man Tankette

During 1927 a further experimental version of the Martel One-Man Tankette was built by Crossley Motors Ltd. Known as the Crossley-Martel One-Man Tankette or Crossley-Martel One-Man Semi-Track Tank, this vehicle consisted of Crossley standard components, with the engine now placed at the rear, and equipped with the Citroën-Kégresse track suspension with which various rubber tracks were tested.

Brief details:

Crew 1
Weight 1.8 tons   **Height** 5 ft 4 in
Length 10 ft   **Engine** 14 hp Crossley
Width 4 ft 9 in   **Max speed** 18.6 mph

Carden-Loyd Machines

Due to the publicity received from the trials of the Martel machine, the firm of Carden-Loyd Tractors Ltd, who had also constructed a cheap light tracked vehicle and exhibited it at Kensington in 1925, approached the War Office for recognition of their enterprise, and the War Office was sufficiently impressed to recommend an order for an experimental machine. As constructed this was a single-seater machine with a box type hull, a Ford engine was situated at the rear, and the driver was placed at the front of the vehicle, with his head and shoulders exposed above the hull. The suspension consisted of 14 small road wheels each side, attached to a frame sprung on coil springs.

The next version to appear was similar in design to the previous model but was now equipped with a small three-

Carden-Loyd One-Man Tankette.

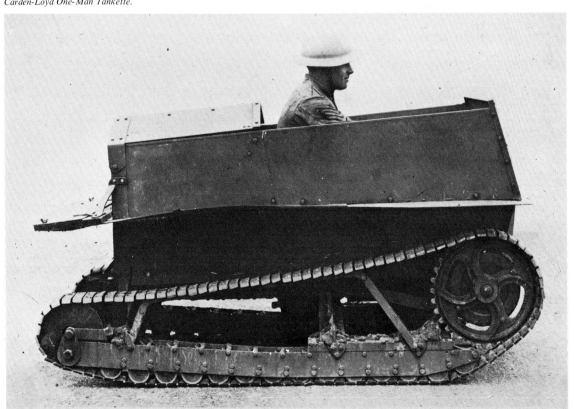

sided turret to protect the driver who was armed with a light automatic rifle. This was designated the Carden-Loyd Mk I.

A modified version of the Mk I, was converted to the wheel and track principle, known as the Mk I*; this had two pneumatic tyred wheels, one either side of the vehicle, and a small steering wheel at the rear. The wheels could be lowered for road running thereby saving wear on the tracks.

Carden-Loyd, Mk I One-Man Tankette.

Brief details:
Crew 1
Weight 1 ton 6 cwt
Length 10 ft 5 in
Width 4 ft 6 in
Height 4 ft 10 in
Engine Ford 4-cylinder Model T, water cooled
Max speed 24 mph (on tracks)   31 mph (on wheels)

The Mk II was again similar in layout to the Mk I, but was now equipped with an improved suspension that consisted of four 10 in soft rubber road wheels per side. A similar version fitted with the wheel and track device became the Mk III.

During 1926, due to the lack of interest in the one-man machines, the firm of Carden-Loyd built a two-man machine, which, while retaining the track and suspension of the One-Man Mk I, was lower and wider to accommodate a second man. No designation was assigned to this vehicle. The second version of a two-man tankette to be built was designated the Mk IV; this was an improved model with a six-sided body, designed for better protection and equipped with a suspension similar to that used on the Mk II. This vehicle was later modified; the track assemblies were fitted with five track rollers strengthened by a supporting bar and it was armed with a ·5 Vickers machine gun.

Carden-Loyd, Mk I* One-Man Tankette.

Though only prototype machines of the previous models had been built and tested by the army it was now decided by the War Office to order from Carden-Loyd a production batch of eight modified two-man machines to be used in a similar role as the Morris Martel vehicles, as scouts with the Experimental Force. Designated Carden-Loyd Mk V, these were basically similar in construction to the Mk IV but were equipped with the wheel and track device. Some of them were later armed with the Vickers ·303 machine gun and tested as machine gun carriers.

With the appearance of the Mk VI machine gun carrier, they were reworked to the Mk VI standard, the wheel and track device being removed. During 1930 one of the vehicles (T 253/MK 8373) underwent considerable alterations, to emerge as a new type of machine. The hull was reshaped, the superstructure had a heightened armoured front and sides and a modified machine gun mount and armoured shield were fitted. Designated Carrier, Machine Gun, Mk V* and nicknamed the "Infighter", this was an attempt to create better crew protection against small arms fire.

Carden-Loyd, Mk II One-Man Tankette.

Brief details:
Crew 2
Weight 1 ton 13 cwt
Length 9 ft 11 in
Width 6 ft 6 in
Height 3 ft 4 in
Engine Ford 4-cylinder Model T, water cooled
Max speed 22 mph (on tracks)   31 mph (on wheels)

Carden-Loyd Two-Man Tankette.

Carden-Loyd, Mk IV Modified.

Carden-Loyd, Mk IV Two-Man Tankette.

Carden-Loyd, Mk V Two-Man Tankette.

Carden-Loyd, Mk V*.

Carden-Loyd, Mk VI machine gun carrier. Early production model.

Carden-Loyd, Mk VI. Equipped with stowage bins.

THE CARDEN-LOYD, MK VI MACHINE GUN CARRIER

The requirements during 1927–1928 for a small turreted reconnaissance vehicle and an armoured machine gun carrier led to the development of the Carden-Loyd Mk VI, which fulfilled the later requirement.

Designed for the role of machine gun carrier, the Mk VI was to become the progenitor of a long line of tracked carriers. Though designed by the firm of Carden-

Loyd, the Mk VI was built by Vickers-Armstrong Ltd who had, at this period, absorbed Carden-Loyd. It was a low two-man vehicle with a body similar in construction to that of the previous Mk IV and Mk V, but with improvements that included an engine enclosed in an asbestos lined box, a protective metal plate over the front differential housing, that had been exposed on the two previous machines, modified tracks and suspension and the fitting of a towing attachment. Improvements were

Carden-Loyd, Mk VI. Late production model.

also made to the Mk VI during production; these included the fitting of stowage bins on either side of the superstructure. This extended to the rear of the vehicle and a new type of track guard that extended down and over the rear sprocket.

Various models of the Mk VI Carrier were developed, to carry the medium machine gun, as a smoke projector carrier, and mortar carrier. In its role of machine gun carrier, the Vickers machine gun could be dismounted from the front of the vehicle and remounted on the tripod that was normally carried on the left front of the vehicle.

This vehicle attracted world-wide attention as a practical low-cost machine, with a performance above the average, and variants of the Mk VI were purchased by various countries, some of them being built under licence. By 1930 the Mk VI Carrier had attained a reasonable mechanical efficiency but due to its moderate fighting capabilities it was relegated in infantry units to the function of a utility tractor and its fighting role abandoned. A fighting role for a carrier with the infantry, however, remained a requirement and since the cavalry were then in the process of mechanisation further uses were therefore contemplated for this type of vehicle, the need for a more suitable machine became paramount. With the appearance of the Vickers machine gun and Bren carriers the Carden-Loyd carrier was obsolete by late 1939.

THE CARDEN-LOYD, MK VI CARRIER AND VARIANTS SUMMARISED

Carrier, Machine Gun, Mk VI

Developed from a series of one- and two-man machine gun carriers or tankettes, the Mk VI was introduced into service during the latter part of 1928 as the standard machine gun carrier. This two-man machine soon achieved popularity as a well designed, and cheap vehicle to build. Various models of the Mk VI were exported abroad, where in some cases they were built under licence, often developing into a considerably different design to the original machine. Examples of this were the Italian versions CV33 and CV35 (Carro Veloce Fast Tank) that were developed from the British model CV29 built under licence. The CV33 and CV35 models were in turn offered for export by Fiat-Ansaldo.

During the period from 1930 to 1932 a little experimental work was done to improve the fighting efficiency of the Mk VI. This took the form of experiments with air-cooled engines, modified suspensions, and better armour protection. Though various prototypes incorporating these improvements were built, interest in this class of vehicle declined and further development was discontinued, not to be revived until 1935.

Brief details:

Crew 2 (driver and gunner)
Weight 1 ton 10 cwt
Armament 1 Vickers .303 machine gun
Armour 6 mm–9 mm
Engine Ford Model T, 22.5 hp
Max speed 28–30 mph (road)

Carden-Loyd, 3.7 in Howitzer Tractor

This was the Mk VI with armament removed, adapted to tow a tracked trailer on which was carried a 3.7 in howitzer.

Carrier, Smoke

This model appeared at the same time as the Mk VI. Basically similar to the machine gun carrier, this version was fitted with smoke-producing equipment, the smoke being discharged from a pipe fixed to the rear of the machine. A small batch of these machines was built.

Carden-Loyd, Mk VI as gun tractor.

Carrier, Smoke.

Carrier, 3 in Mortar.

Carrier, 3 in Mortar modified.

Carrier, 60 mm Mortar.

Carrier, 3 in Mortar

This machine was similar in design to the Mk VI machine gun carrier, but had a 3 in mortar mounted on the left of the front deck for close-support work with light tanks. The mortar could be fired from the vehicle, but was usually dismounted for firing.

Brief details:

Crew 2
Weight 1 ton 7 cwt
Armament 3 in Stokes Mortar
Engine Ford Model T, 22.5 hp
Max speed 25 mph (road)

Carden-Loyd Carrier, 47 mm gun.

Other variants of mortar carriers existed, however. One version, a normal Mk VI, had the front superstructure altered to allow the infantry mortar, baseplate and bipod to be stowed on the front deck. In the rearmoured roof half-way across the crew's compartment; later version, built to carry a 60 mm mortar, had an armoured roof half-way across the crews' compartment; this was flush with the vehicle sides. The mortar was carried in a box fixed to the front of the vehicle, other equipment being stowed inside the vehicle.

Carden-Loyd, Carrier, 47 mm Gun

This was an adaptation of the 47 mm infantry gun to the Mk VI carrier, the gun and shield being mounted on the front of the vehicle. The mounting was of a special type and could be modified to take any gun of the approximate size of the 47 mm gun. Number of 47 mm rounds carried was 100.

Carden-Loyd, 20 mm Gun Tractor

This was the Mk VI mortar version, with the mortar removed, the vehicle being used as a tractor to tow a tracked trailer containing four men and equipment. Behind the trailer was towed the 20 mm (0.8 in) Oerlikon gun which was carried on a tracked mount. The object of this combination was to obtain an effective anti-tank gun and crew which could be easily transported across country.

It must be remembered that at this period, the early 'thirties, spending on military equipment in Britain was very limited indeed and only very small numbers of these types were built for troop trials.

Carden-Loyd, Mk VI, with Armoured Tops

This version had two pyramid shaped hinged head covers covering the fighting compartment but was otherwise similar to the standard Mk VI. Built in 1930 this version was supplied to various countries, including Siam, USSR, Japan and Italy. One model was also supplied to the Air Ministry in 1931.

Carrier, Machine Gun, Mk VI (Indian Pattern)

Two special models of this type (B11E3 and B11E4) were produced during 1929. With these machines, the hull, engine, transmission and suspension were unaltered, but special arrangements were made to render these machines more suitable for use in hot climates. This included a modified cooling system with slot radiator and larger fan, a canvas canopy erected over the crew's compartment as a protection against the sun

Carden-Loyd, Mk VI with Armoured tops.

Carrier, Machine Gun, Mk VI Indian Pattern.

Carrier, Machine Gun, Mk VI Experimental.

and various other devices in the form of asbestos lagging, etc, to ensure increased comfort for the crew.

Carrier, Machine Gun, Mk VI, Experimental (B11E6)

This version, built in 1929 (T608/MT9905) was basically the Mk VI with a modified superstructure and heavier and wider track, with the addition of two return rollers instead of the normal fixed rail guide.

Carrier, Machine Gun, Mk VIa

Two experimental machines (B11E1 and B11E2) were fitted with 25 hp Armstrong-Siddeley air-cooled engines and delivered during 1930. These were similar to the standard Mk VI vehicle in size, but were about 12 cwt

heavier, their total weight being 1 ton 18 cwt. The exhaust system was trunked in and the crew were protected from the heat of the engine. The hull was of mild steel plate 9 mm throughout. The front, back and side superstructure plates were sloped and heightened to protect the crews' heads, and an access door was fitted in the front glacis plate. Alterations to the suspension included provision of two return rollers with rubber tyres instead of the normal fixed rail guard, heavy duty tracks, and idler wheel. Extension mudguards were fitted to the rear wings. One of these machines, B11E2, was sent to Egypt for trials. During 1931 a further vehicle with an improved type of air-cooled engine was produced. This carried the designation Mk VIa (B11E7). The two experimental vehicles B11E1 and B11E2 and the Mk VIa (B11E7) were all subsequently classified under the designation Carrier Machine Gun Mk VIa.

Carrier, Machine Gun, Mk VIb

Ten machine gun carriers with air-cooled engines were built by the Royal Ordnance Factory in 1932 (T908–T917). These were an improved type of Mk VIa and were, in fact, at first known as "Mk VIa, Improved Type". This was later changed to Mk VIb. These vehicles were fitted with a modified exhaust system, intended to reduce the noise and fumes. The superstructure was again modified to increase the protection for the crew, and a modified form of machine gun mounting with a shield

was fitted, the machine gun tripod being carried at the rear of the vehicle. The suspension was also altered, the rear idler wheels being lowered to give a longer track contour which relieved the tendency to pitch. Five of these vehicles were sent to Egypt for trials.

Carrier, Machine Gun, Mk VI*

Two vehicles T1010 (MT9792/B11E8) and T1011 (MT9793/B11E9) built during 1932. These two vehicles were fitted with a Model A Ford Engine and gearbox. The Model A engine was four-cylinder unit rated at 24 hp, and developed a maximum brake hp at 2,200 rpm. In general construction the Mk VI* was similar to the Mk VIa and was fitted with a $7\frac{1}{2}$ in track.

Carrier, Machine Gun, Mk VIA.

Carrier, Machine Gun, Mk VIB.

Carrier, Machine Gun, 3-Man

This was an experimental machine (T991/B11E10) built during 1933, having a heightened superstructure and adapted to carry three men. The suspension was similar to that of the Mk VIb but with only one return roller. The exhaust system was placed outside the machine on the left, running from the front of the vehicle to the rear.

Brief details:

Crew 3
Armament 1 Vickers .303 machine gun
Engine Ford 24 hp water cooled
Max speed 18 mph

Light Armoured Vehicle, Mk VI*

Modified versions of this model were exported to Siam, Bolivia, Japan and other countries. Fitted with a Model BB Ford engine, this vehicle had complete overhead covering, consisting of bevelled hinged flaps that opened to the front and rear. An access door was fitted in the rear of the vehicle.

1 *Early type of Light Armoured Vehicle, Mk VI*.
2 *Light Armoured Vehicle, Mk VI*.
3 *Carrier, Machine Gun, 3-Man.*

Crossley improvised armoured tender.

Lancia armoured tender.

Peerless armoured tender.

PART FOUR
MISCELLANEOUS CARRIERS, 1922–1934

Armoured Tenders

During the period of the Irish Troubles 1916–1922, it became necessary to use protected vehicles for street patrols and internal security. Early vehicles used in this role were of an improvised type with makeshift armour, but later a standardised form of protection was designed that consisted of an armoured cab and radiator and an armoured box type superstructure fitted with a V-shaped wire netting roof for protection against stones or grenades. Some of the hulls were slotted for the use of

rifles. Vehicles used as armoured tenders included Lancia and Crossley trucks, Peerless lorries were also used, these being conversions from the role of mobile mounts for the 3 in AA gun. Some of these armoured tenders were allocated to the army, but most of them eventually reached the hands of the Royal Ulster Constabulary.

Armstrong-Siddeley, Full Tracked, Armoured Machine Gun Carrier

This was an experimental light type of Dragon (gun tower), designed and made by Messrs Armstrong-Siddeley in 1924. By means of pivoting front horns and a

25

laterally flexed track, steering was possible without skidding or braking. The vehicle was adapted to carry two Vickers machine guns on pedestal mounts for use against ground or air targets.

Brief details:
Crew 8 men fully equipped
Weight 3 tons
Engine Armstrong-Siddeley 30 hp water cooled
Max speed 12 mph (road) 8 mph (cross country)

Carrier, Machine Gun, No. 1

This was first designed as a three-man light tank in 1925 by the Royal Ordnance Factory. It embodied an effort to reduce the cost of manufacture by utilising a commercial type of engine, in this case, an omnibus engine and a cheap type of cast steel track. Based on a suspension similar to that of the Vickers Medium Tank, the vehicle carried two small machine gun turrets, one situated at the front of the vehicle, to the left of the driver's hatch, and a second placed at the rear.

Conceived under the code name A3E1 Light Tank, this was later changed to Carrier, Machine Gun, No. 1.

Brief details:
Crew 3
Weight 6.14 tons
Engine AEC 40 hp water cooled
Max speed 16 mph

Carrier, Machine Gun, Armoured 30 cwt, Burford-Kégresse

Built in 1926, this was a semi-tracked vehicle of the type then in use as field artillery tractors, and was adapted as a machine gun carrier by being equipped with an armoured body and one or two Vickers machine guns on modified Scarff aircraft mountings which could be used against air or ground targets. Developed as support weapons for cavalry or infantry, a small production batch was built.

Brief details:
Crew 2
Weight 3 tons 17 cwt
Armament 2 Vickers machine guns
Engine Burford M29 hp 4-cylinder water cooled
Max speed 20 mph (road) 10 mph (cross country)

Carrier, Machine Gun, 1 Ton Morris

This was the Carrier, GS Morris, a one-ton semi-tracked load carrier, with an experimental pedestal mount fitted with twin Lewis machine guns. Unarmoured, this vehicle was received for trials in 1926.

1

1 *Carrier, Machine Gun, No 1.*
2 *Armstrong-Siddeley, Full Tracked Armoured Machine Gun Carrier.*
3 *Carrier, Machine Gun, No 1 rear view.*
4 *Carrier, Machine Gun, 1 ton Morris.*
5 *Carrier, Machine Gun, Armoured, 30 cwt Burford-Kégresse rear view.*
6 *Carrier, Machine Gun, Armoured, 30 cwt Burford-Kégresse.*

4

5

6

Crossley, 6-Wheeled, Machine Gun Carrier

An experimental type built in 1928 for carrying two Vickers machine guns and crews. The chassis was the standard BGV2 Crossley light six-wheeled lorry with a special body that had been designed and constructed by the War Department. Unarmoured, it was designed to be low and as inconspicuous as possible. Overall tracks were carried for the two pairs of rear wheels for use over soft ground.

Tractor, One-Man Machine Gun Carrier

Built in 1934, this was a Vickers-Carden-Loyd Utility Tractor adapted to the role of a one-man machine gun carrier. Armoured only on the front section with $\frac{1}{4}$ in steel plate, the tractor carried a Vickers-Berthier automatic rifle on a specially designed quick release mount.

Tractor, Light, GS

This was a modified version of the Utility tractor equipped with hinged sheet steel sides. Introduced as load carriers to replace horse drawn transport, this vehicle was capable of carrying a load of 8 cwt and towing a two-wheeled GS limber containing 13 cwt. Used as supply vehicles and carriers of Vickers and Lewis machine gun sections, in which role they were eventually replaced by the Vickers Machine Gun Carrier. Two versions of this tractor were built, Tractor, Light, GS Mk I and Tractor, Light, GS Mk Ia (HS) High Speed.

PART FIVE
THE MACHINE GUN
SCOUT AND BREN CARRIERS

The next stage in the carrier development was begun in 1934 when, as a commercial project, Vickers-Armstrong Ltd developed a machine, the VA D50, that could be adapted for the roles of either a tractor for a light field gun or as a machine gun carrier. During 1935 it was decided by the War Office to purchase two modified machines for trials, one of them as a proposed replacement for the Carden-Loyd Mk VI Machine Gun Carrier.

With the original conception of a vehicle as a machine gun carrier, it was required that it should have a driver, gunner and machine gun in an armoured front, thus being able to return fire as it advanced. It was also required to carry a machine gun team consisting of four men, machine gun, tripod and ammunition, able to leave and operate independently of the carrier. The machine, built by Vickers-Armstrong Ltd, was constructed to these specifications; the compartment for the driver and front machine gunner consisted of an armoured box and positioned centrally behind this was the engine which was protected by steel hinged plates mounted on a frame. Seating accommodation for the independent machine gun unit was arranged on either side of the engine, collapsible armoured sides were provided that acted as

Tractor, One-Man Machine Gun Carrier.

Tractor, Light. GS.

Carrier, Machine Gun, Crossley.

back-rests and as protection for the independent unit.

This vehicle, of which only one was built, was designated the Experimental Carrier, Machine Gun (WD No T1583) (BMM.939).

In the next version to appear of this class of machine the crew was reduced to three with just the front machine gun. The folding armoured sides were dispensed with and the left side of the vehicle superstructure was now made a fixture forming a compartment for the third member of the crew. The right side of the vehicle was left open and used for stowage. Other modifications to this machine included the fitting of air ducts either side of the engine and the enclosing of the front headlamps in steel boxes. Designated Carrier Machine Gun No 1, Mk I, a small batch of these machines were built in mild steel (WD Nos T1828–T1840, T1921). Six of these machines were later converted as pilot models for Carrier, Machine Gun No 2 Mk I, Cavalry Mk I and Scout Mk I; the remaining vehicles being used as instructional machines.

Early in 1937 Carrier Machine Gun No 2, Mk I appeared. This was basically similar to Carrier No 1 Mk I, but with many improvements. The front Vickers machine gun was now mounted in an armoured housing, the engine air ducts had been modified, the steel boxes on the front headlamps had been removed and a stowage box had been installed on the right side of the vehicle. The superstructure on the left side of the carrier had been improved and an armoured folding back-rest was fitted for the third man's protection and comfort.

After Vickers-Armstrong had built a batch of these machines (WD Nos T2294–T2336) their work on this class of machine ceased and other firms undertook production. These included Thornycroft (T2531–T2621), Morris (T2832–T2982), Aveling Barford (T3231–T3291), and Sentinel Wagon (T3716–T3915). Primarily built to carry a medium machine gun, the carrier was again modified late in 1938 to mount the Bren Light Machine Gun. This was due to the adoption by the British Army of this Czech designed weapon. The gun housing was adapted for this light machine gun with consequent alteration to other equipment. Some of these vehicles were also fitted with the Boys anti-tank rifle. These carriers, and the Carriers Machine Gun No 2, Mk I that were modified and rearmed with the Bren

Carrier, VA D50 mounting two Vickers machine guns.

LMG were now designated Carriers, Bren, No 2, Mks I and II.

The pilot model of the Bren Carrier, a reworked Carrier MG No 2, Mk I, was converted by Thornycroft who with various other firms undertook production of this vehicle. Production was also begun in Australia and New Zealand by 1941 and ended in 1943 after a total of 5,501 machines had been built in these two countries. The Australian version was welded whereas those produced in Britain were of riveted construction.

Prior to the outbreak of the war, two variants of the carrier appeared, based on the Bren Carrier. These special variants were developed for the carrying of personnel and for reconnaissance. The Cavalry Carrier of which only 50 were built (by Nuffield) was designed to carry the dismounted personnel of the Cavalry light tank regiments in the mobile (mechanised) division. They had accommodation for the driver and six men but were armoured only in front. The Scout Carrier was very similar to the MG or Bren Carriers but carried either an extra man or a wireless set. These had a Boys anti-tank rifle mounted in the front, and sockets in the rear compartment for the Bren gun. These vehicles were designed for use with the infantry scout elements and reconnaissance troops in the mechanised divisional cavalry regiments, and their full designations were Carrier, Cavalry, Mk I and Carrier, Scout, Mk I. A third variant was developed soon after the outbreak of the war in 1939 for use with the Royal Artillery as an armoured observation post and known as Carrier, Armoured OP, Mks I and II.

Experimental Machine Gun Carrier, VA D50.

THE MACHINE GUN, SCOUT AND BREN CARRIERS SUMMARISED

Experimental Machine Gun Carrier, VA D50

This was an experimental Vickers machine that was tested in 1935 as a Machine Gun Carrier or Light Dragon. The vehicle was fitted with a Horstmann type suspension with two return rollers per side. The driver and front machine gunner were in an armoured compartment, and seating accommodation with folding bench type backs was provided either side of the vehicle behind the driver's position for an independent machine gun unit or field gun crew. This vehicle was also tested with two Vickers .303 machine guns, mounted one above the other in the front gunner's compartment.

Tractor with 40 mm Equipment.

Machine Gun Carrier, Experimental (Armoured).

Machine Gun Carrier, Experimental (Armoured) rear view.

Carrier, Machine Gun, No 1, Mk I.

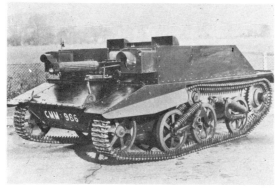

Carrier, Machine Gun, No 1, Mk I. Fitted with armoured shield on machine gun.

Carrier, Machine Gun, No 2, Mk I.

Carrier equipped with QF 2 pdr anti-tank gun.

Carrier, Machine Gun, No 2, Mk I rear view.

Machine Gun Carrier, Experimental (Armoured)

This vehicle was designed to carry a driver, front machine-gunner and an independent machine gun unit of four men. The independent unit were seated on benches placed left and right side of the vehicle behind the driver's compartment. The vehicle's rear sides were fitted with two folding armoured sides to give protection to the machine gun unit, and these folded down inwards when not in use. Stowage bins were fitted both sides of the hull front. Engine was a Ford V-8. (WD/Reg No T1583/BMM939).

40 mm SP (Tractor with 40 mm Equipment)

Tested as a self-propelled mount for a 40 mm gun, this conversion used the VA D50 chassis on which several changes had been made, including the reduction to one return roller per side. The gun was mounted behind the driver's compartment, having a 360° traverse.

Carrier, Machine Gun, No 1, Mk I

Developed by Vickers from the experimental machine gun carrier and introduced into service in 1936, this was the prototype of the carriers of the Machine Gun and Bren series. With the appearance of this vehicle the idea of carrying an independent machine gun crew was now abandoned, the crew being reduced to three. A small batch of these machines was built. The hull was of mild steel throughout and the left side of the vehicle was now built up to form a compartment for the third member of the crew, the right side being used for stowage. Some vehicles fitted with small armoured shield on machine gun.

Brief details:
Crew 3
Weight 3.15 tons
Armament 1 .303 Vickers machine gun
Armour 10 mm basis
Engine Ford V-8 30 bhp liquid cooled

Carrier, Machine Gun, No 2, Mk I

Introduced into service during 1937, this version was basically similar to the Carrier No 1, Mk I, but with improvements to the superstructure and machine gun housing. These vehicles were later equipped with the Bren LMG and/or with the Boys anti-tank rifle replacing the Vickers .303 machine gun, and reworked to Bren carrier standards.

Carrier, equipped with QF 2 pdr Anti-Tank Gun

Developed during 1938, this was a Carrier MG No 2, Mk I, fitted with a 2 pounder Mk IX or Mk X anti-tank gun mounted above the engine and arranged to fire to the front through a fixed shield. Ammunition was carried in racks on the off-side of the gun. Crew was 4 and weight was 3.9 tons. (WD/Reg No T2335/FME890).

Carrier, Bren, No 2, Mks I and II

Entering service in 1938, the Bren Carrier was similar in design to the Carrier, MG No 2, Mk I, but with improved armour protection, modified machine gun housing, and other various modifications. Issued to British infantry, on the scale of ten per battalion, they first saw action in France and the Low Countries during 1939–1940. WD numbers as follows: T2622–T2831, T2983–T3230, T3292–T3425, T4349–T4384, T4515–T4664, T4716–T5084, T5883–T5908.

Brief details:

Crew 3
Weight 3.75 tons
Armament .303 Bren LMG or Boys anti-tank rifle
Engine Ford V-8 85 bhp liquid cooled
Speed 30 mph

Carrier, Scout, Mk I

Introduced into service in 1938, the general construction of the hull, etc, was similar to the Bren Carriers, but provision was made for carrying a No 11 wireless set, the batteries for which were stored in a bullet-proof box housed on the rear axle cover plate. The openings in the rear of the engine cover were covered with wire screens to eliminate interference with the wireless. On these vehicles, the built-up superstructure was reversed, except on the pilot model T1834/CMM990. The Scout Carrier was intended to be used by divisional mechanised cavalry, together with Light Tanks, as scout machines. WD numbers: T3966–T4165, T4485–T4514, T5255–T5550, T5616–T5756.

Brief details:

Crew 3–4
Weight 3.3 tons
Armament 1 Boys anti-tank rifle and Bren LMG

Carrier, Cavalry, Mk I

Designed as a personnel carrier, intended for use with the cavalry light tank regiments to carry the dismounted personnel, this vehicle differed in detail from the Bren Carrier. Seating accommodation was arranged for six men in addition to the driver and gunner, benches being provided either side of the vehicle behind the driver's compartment. A metal frame was fitted to carry a

Carrier, Bren, No 2, Mks I and II.

canvas hood to provide protection against the weather. The engine cover was of a modified design, having sliding access doors and a louvre at the rear. These machines were only armoured around the driver's compartment. Brief details as for Bren Carrier. WD numbers: T3916–T3965.

Carrier, Armoured, OP, No 1, Mk I

Designed for use with the Royal Artillery as a mobile armoured observation post, the hull construction was basically the same as the Scout Carrier with a few modifications, the principal one being the provision of an adjustable shutter in the machine gun housing in lieu of the gun aperture. This was to permit the use of binoculars. These machines were fitted with a No 11 wireless set, a cable drum being fitted to the rear of the vehicle. The engine cover was the same as fitted to the Scout Carrier. Vehicle was equipped with a Bren LMG. WD numbers: T5984–T6078.

General Service Vehicle

Tested in 1937, this was the early Carrier Machine Gun, Experimental (BMM939) with a converted superstructure. Around the top of the front gunner's compartment was fitted a grooved rail in which was enclosed a four-wheeled pinion mount carrying a Boys anti-tank rifle. The gunner was able to use this travelling mount to traverse the gun from the front to the side of the vehicle. A Bren LMG was carried in the normal machine gun housing.

Carrier, Bren, No 2, Mks I and II side view.

Smith Gun (Bren SP)

The Smith 3 inch smooth bore gun or projector was one of several types of weapon evolved for the use of the British Home Guard during the "invasion scare" period of 1940–41. Normally carried on a two-wheeled carriage, a conversion of this weapon existed where the gun was mounted on the front of a Bren Carrier on which the superstructure had been heightened and modified. The gun was in a sponson type of mounting, had a limited traverse, and fired two types of projectiles, anti-personnel (weighing 8 lb) and anti-tank (weighing 6 lb). Range of the gun was 300 yards. At this period individual Home Guard units built themselves a variety of extemporised armoured vehicles, mostly on car chassis, and it is believed that the Smith gun on a modified Bren Gun Carrier was built at Ford Motor Co Dagenham for a Home Guard Unit.

Carrier, Scout, Mk I.

General Service Vehicle.

Smith Gun (Bren SP).

Carrier, Cavalry, Mk I.

PART SIX
THE UNIVERSAL CARRIER AND ASSOCIATED VEHICLES

It was considered uneconomic and unnecessary to build separate versions of a basic machine to fulfil a variety of roles, so consequently in 1940 a Universal type of carrier was produced for all purposes, with special requirements met by minor modifications. Designated Carrier, Universal, Mk I, II and III, this vehicle remained the standard combat carrier throughout the war.

The general construction of the hull was a combination of both Bren and Scout Carrier, but with protection plates on both sides and at the rear, the previous machines only having armour plate on one side of the vehicle. The engine cover was of a modified design having bullet-proof plates on top only, the side plates being of mild steel and easily detachable. Angular mud deflectors were fitted on the front track guards, and two rear steps were fitted, one each side of the vehicle. A crew of three was carried, two in the front compartment, the driver and gunner, with a third man seated in the rear right-hand side of the hull. The main weapon fitted in the gun housing varied, and was either a .55 in Boys anti-tank rifle, a .303 in Bren LMG, or even a Vickers .303 in medium machine gun (this latter was common practice on Australian carriers). When the Bren LMG was fitted in the machine gun housing the vehicle was sometimes erroneously called a Bren Carrier.

These vehicles were often re-armed in the field to suit users' requirements and were fitted with a variety of weapons, which included: .30 in Browning MG, .50 in Browning MG, German 20 mm Solothurn anti-tank gun. These weapons were usually mounted on pintle sockets in the rear compartment. Light weapons like the PIAT were sometimes fitted in the front compartment.

Several carrier units, to achieve extra fire-power, mounted the 2 in mortar on the engine cover of their carriers. The desirability of mounting these mortars as vehicle equipment for certain roles led to the preparation of a design of mounting to be fitted in the gunner's compartment. This became a standard fitting in 1943, being included in all Universals of Mk II standard. The stowage arrangement of equipment in the carrier depended on the role that the carrier was to undertake, eg, Scout or Infantry carrier, etc.

Used initially in the Western Desert and subsequently in all campaigns in all theatres of war, Universal Carriers were supplied to all Allied armies (Russia receiving 200) except the USA. The Carrier Universal Mk I designation covered also the Bren and Scout Carriers that were converted to Universal standard. Apart from improvements in design the only wartime developments were the production of specially modified versions, the Artillery OP Carrier, 3 in Mortar Carrier and carrier for flame-throwing equipment. Provision was made for the fitting of a No 11 wireless set.

Brief details:
Crew 3
Weight 4 to 4½ tons
Armament 1 × .55 in Boys Anti-Tank Rifle or 1 × .303 in Bren LMG
Armour 7–10 mm basis
Engine Ford V-8 65 bhp
Speed 30 mph
Provision was made for the fitting of a No. 11 wireless set

The demand for the Universal Carrier far exceeded the capacity of the United Kingdom and production was

undertaken by Australia who supplied their own army and shipped 1,500 to China; Canada who built 33,987, supplying more than a fifth of the British Carrier needs and New Zealand where a small batch was built for home use. In addition to the production of the Universal Carriers both Canada and the United States undertook experimental vehicle work in the hope of designing a more satisfactory vehicle, it being an accepted fact that the Universal was overloaded and underpowered. In the USA the result was the T16, basically the Universal with a larger chassis, four bogie wheels and a larger engine. The original vehicle was designated Cargo Carrier T16 but was redesignated Universal Carrier T16 for the sake of uniformity with British nomenclature. It was designed in 1942 partly for British requirements and partly for US Army operations against the Japanese. The British were supplied with 2,625 T16s in 1944 and 604 in 1945. The T16 was not considered entirely satisfactory by the

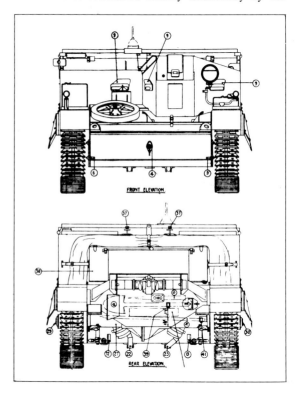

FRONT ELEVATION.

REAR ELEVATION.

Carrier, Universal No 1, Mk I.

Carrier, Universal No 1, Mk I rear view.

Carrier, Universal No 3, Mk I (Canadian).*

Carrier. Universal No 2, Mk II (Carrier Platoon, Infantry Batt).

Carrier, Universal No 2, Mk II rear view.

Carrier, Universal No 2, Mk II (Carrier, Scout, Motor Batt. equipped with W/T).

British General Staff, in spite of its many improvements over the Universal, as it was mechanically unreliable and had a pay-load even smaller than the Universal. A modified version, the T16E2, was projected and built late in 1945, which had altered bogie spacing to reduce track wear. Few of these T16 vehicles were used by the British operationally.

In Canada a much more promising machine known as the Windsor was introduced in 1943 by the Ford Motor Co of Windsor. Although this vehicle incorporated 90% Loyd Carrier components its design was based on that of the Universal Carrier, but it was much larger and more powerful. It was specially intended to replace the Loyd Carrier as a gun towing vehicle but was so satisfactory in early trials that its use was seriously considered in the role of the Universal Carrier. Due to mechanical trouble after the design had been approved and production had begun (at the rate of 500 a month), the Windsor was only in service in small numbers by the end of the war as a towing vehicle for the 6 pdr anti-tank gun with 21 Army Group.

The Different Marks of the Universal Carrier Produced in England and Canada are Summarised below:

Carrier, Universal, No 2, Mk I
Similar to Mk I, but with an American built Ford V-8, 85 bhp GAEA engine.

Carrier, Universal, No 2A, Mk I
As for Mk I, but with the American built Ford V-8, 85 bhp GAE engine.

Carrier, Universal, No 3, Mk I*
As for Mk I, but built in Canada with a Ford V-8 85 bhp engine.

Carrier, Universal, No 1, Mk II
This model resulted from an attempt to improve the original Universal and featured a welded water-proofed hull and new type of stowage arrangement. This latter varied with the role of the carrier, ie, Scout Carrier of Motor Battalion, Platoon Carrier of Infantry Battalion, etc. It was fitted with a 4 in smoke discharger

Carrier, Universal No 1, Mk III.

Carrier, Universal No 1, Mk III rear.

Carrier, Universal No 3, Mk II*.

Firing the 2 in mortar from the engine cover.

Universal Carrier fitted with .50 Browning machine gun in front compartment.

This vehicle is armed with the German 20 mm Solothurn anti-tank gun.

This Canadian Carrier has been armed with the Besa machine gun.

Carrier armed with the German MG 42 and the Vickers K gun.

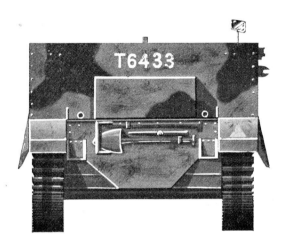

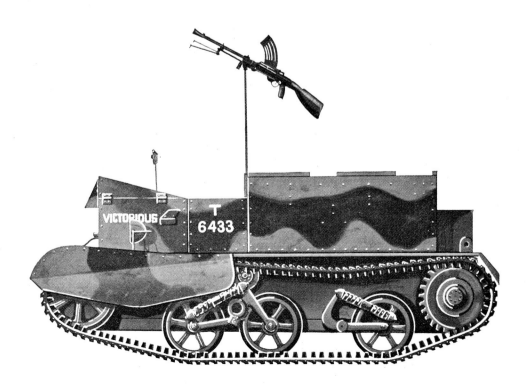

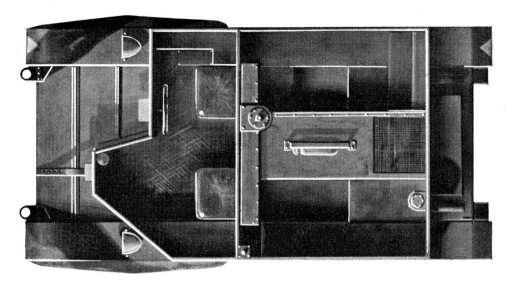

Universal Carrier No. 1, Mk I of Training Battalion, Grenadier Guards, Catterick, September, 1940.

Universal Carrier No. 1, Mk I Battalion Commander's vehicle of 4th Battalion, Dorsetshire Regiment, 43rd (Wessex) Division, October, 1942.

Artwork drawn by Martin Lee
© Profile Publications Limited.

generator or a 2 in mortar on the left side of the gunner's compartment. The front quarter of the track run was totally enclosed by a valance. Four foot steps were fitted, two each side of the vehicle, and a spare wheel and tow rope was carried on the front of the vehicle, a large kit was also carried across the rear of the hull, and brackets for water and oil cans were fitted to the front track guards.

Brief details:
Crew 4
Weight 4 tons 10 cwt
Armament 1 Boys anti-tank rifle or Bren LMG
Armour 7–10 mm basis
Engine Ford V-8 85 bhp
Max speed 30 mph

Carrier, Universal, No 2, Mk II
As for Carrier No 1, Mk II, but equipped with an American built Ford V-8 85 bhp GAE engine.

Carrier, Universal, No 2A, Mk II
As for No 1 Mk II, but with American built Ford V-8 85 bhp GAEA engine.

Carrier, Universal, No 3, Mk II*
As for No 1, Mk II, but built in Canada.

Carrier, Universal, No 1, Mk III
This was a further attempt to improve the Universal Carrier, this model retained the welded hull of the Mk II, but now had a modified air inlet and engine cover. Basic details were the same as the Mk II.

Carrier, Universal, No 2, Mk III
As for Mk III, but with the American built Ford V-8 85 bhp GAE engine.

Carrier, Universal, No 2A, Mk III
As for Mk III, but with the American built Ford V-8 85 bhp GAEA engine.

Canadian Universal Carriers in service with Red Army.

Carrier, Universal, No 3, Mk III*
As for the Mk III, but built in Canada.

All Ford V-8 engines of 221 cubic inch capacity (85 bhp) of American, Canadian or British production, less their ancillary equipment like carburettors, electrical fittings, etc, were basically interchangeable as an assembly in any Mk/Type of Loyd or Universal Carrier manufactured to the Canadian or British Specification.

Typical WD numbers for the Universal Carrier Mk I are given here though this listing is not exhaustive.

British built
T6079–T6728; T7441–T8090; T8120–T8419; T8420–T9095; T10678–T11677; T11678–T12677; T12678–T13677; T13678–T14677; T20494–T21893; T21954–T22653; T28141–T28840.

Canadian built
Canadian War Department vehicles had the prefix CT rather than the 'T'
CT22654–CT22703; CT28841–CT29790; CT36021–CT37120; CT41469–CT42868; CT42869–CT43651; CT49250–CT58134; CT49184–CT59683

Universal Carrier of the Czechoslovak forces fighting with the Red Army.

MG CARRIERS

One serious drawback of the carrier was its lack of heavy armament, and many units overcame this by the unofficial adoption of assorted weapons. While the Vickers machine gun had been carried in the front sponson of the early Machine Gun Carriers of 1935–37 and later mounted unofficially in this fashion by some British carrier units in the war years, this type of mounting gave only a limited field of fire. When during 1943 it was decided to reintroduce the Vickers medium machine gun in the Motor Machine Gun Battalions a new arrangement was decided on. The gun was now sited behind the driver's compartment on a pedestal mount which was fitted on a strengthened engine cover. This position allowed an all round field of fire. The gun could also be dismounted and fired from a tripod that was carried stowed on the vehicle. A crew of four was carried. The various vehicles used for carrying medium machine guns (MMG) were designated as follows:

Carrier, Medium Machine Gun, No 1, Mk I
This was the original Universal Carrier, Mk I, adapted for the MMG role.

Carrier, Medium Machine Gun, No 2, Mk I
The Universal Carrier, Mk I (American engine) adpated for the MMG role.

Carrier, Medium Machine Gun, No 2A, Mk I
The Universal Carrier, Mk I (American engine) adapted for MMG role.

Carrier, Medium Machine Gun, No 3, Mk I*
Universal Carrier, Mk I* (Canadian production) adapted for MMG role.

Carrier, Medium Machine Gun, No 1 Mk II
Universal Carrier, Mk II, adapted for MMG role.

Carrier, Medium Machine Gun, No 2, Mk II
Universal Carrier, Mk II (American engine) adapted for MMG role.

Carrier, Medium Machine Gun, No 2A, Mk II
Universal Carrier, Mk II (American engine) adapted for MMG role.

Carrier, Medium Machine Gun, No 3, Mk II*
Universal Carrier, Mk II* (Canadian production) adapted for MMG role.

Other than their change of role and altered armament and stowage arrangements, all the MMG carriers had the same mechanical and physical characteristics as the Universal Carriers from which they were converted.

Carrier, Medium Machine Gun, No 3 Mk I*.

Carrier, Medium Machine Gun, No 1 Mk II.

Post-war line up of a section of the MMG Platoon of the 1st Batt Scots Guards.

Carrier, Armoured. OP, No 1, Mk II.

Carrier, Armoured. OP, No 1, Mk II rear.

Carrier, Armoured. OP, No 1, Mk IIIw rear.

Carrier, Armoured. OP, No 1, Mk IIIw.

OP CARRIERS

For the Artillery, the Universal Carrier was developed in a modified form as a command and observation vehicle. The different OP (Observation Post) models produced are outlined and described below. The Mk I was based on the Scout Carrier.

Carrier, Armoured, OP, No 1, Mk II

Hull construction was as for the Universal Carrier Mk I, except that an adjustable shutter was fitted in the front gun housing. The engine cover was slightly modified from that on the Universal Carrier. A wireless set No 11 was standard equipment. A crew of three was carried consisting of a driver and observer (with telephone) in the front compartment, and a radio operator in the rear to operate the No 11 wireless set. A drum of telephone cable was fitted to the rear of the vehicle. Specimen WD numbers for these vehicles were: T17107–T17359, T35528–T36020, T46782–T47097. Some vehicles were modified to carry both No 11 and No 18 wireless sets.

Carrier, Armoured, OP, No 1, Mk IIIw

This was based on the Universal Carrier Mk III, and was similar to the Mk II OP, but with a welded instead of riveted hull. A crew of four and additional wireless equipment was carried in this version. Two cable drums were fitted, one in the front and one at the rear. WD numbers: T84621–T88063.

Carrier, Armoured, OP, No 2, Mk III

This corresponded to the Universal Carrier No 2, Mk III. It was equipped as for the OP No 1, Mk III. It had the Ford V-8 85 bhp GAE engine.

Carrier, 3 in Mortar, No 1, Mk I

Carrier, Armoured, OP, No 2A, Mk III
Equipped as for the OP, No 1, Mk III, this was based on the Universal Carrier No 2A, Mk III, with Ford V-8 85 bhp GAEA engine.

Carrier, Armoured, OP, No 3, Mk III*
Equipped as for the OP No 1, Mk III version, this was based on the Canadian-built Universal Carrier No 1, Mk III*.

THE 3 IN MORTAR CARRIER

In 1942 the Universal Carrier was adapted for the transport of the 3 in mortar, ammunition and crew. The mortar, bipod and base-plate were carried secured at the rear of the vehicle, and the mortar ammunition was stowed inside the carrier, contained in racks either side of the vehicle. The mortar and crew were transported to their firing position, where they dismounted and assembled the weapon for action. Though not a normal practice, the mortar in some cases was assembled in the front gunner's compartment and fired from there. The various models of mortar carrier produced are described here.

Carrier, 3 in Mortar, No 1, Mk I
Basically Carrier Universal Mk I adapted for the mortar role, this vehicle carried a crew of five with driver and front gunner in the front compartment, two men in the rear right-hand side of the hull, and one man in the left rear side. A spare wheel was fitted on the front of the vehicle and a wire tow rope, shovel and pick was carried at the rear. The rear stowage box was removed and brackets were provided in its place to hold the mortar parts.

Carrier Mortar section in action.

Carrier, 3 in Mortar, No 1, Mk I rear.

Carrier, 3 in Mortar, No 2, Mk I

As for No 1, Mk I, but with a Ford V-8, 85 bhp HAE engine.

Carrier, 3 in Mortar, No 2A, Mk I

As for No 1, Mk I but with a Ford V-8, 85 bhp GAEA engine.

Carrier, 3 in Mortar, No 3, Mk I*

As for No 1, Mk I but with a Ford V-8 85 bhp engine and built in Canada.

Carrier, 3 in Mortar, No 1, Mk II

Basically a Carrier Universal Mk II adapted for the mortar role, this version carried the same crew as the Mk I but no spare wheel was fitted and the tow rope was now carried at the front. Footsteps were added to the sides of the vehicle and were the main distinguishing feature of this mark.

Carrier, 3 in Mortar, No 2, Mk II

As for No 1, Mk II, but with a Ford V-8 85 bhp GAE engine.

Carrier, 3 in Mortar, No 2A, Mk II

As for No 1, Mk II, but with a Ford V-8 85 bhp GAEA engine.

Carrier, 3 in Mortar, No 3, Mk II*

As for No 1, Mk II, but with a Ford V-8 85 bhp engine and built in Canada.

FLAME-THROWER CARRIERS

Late in 1940 experiments were carried out with a flame-projecting cylinder that had been evolved as a static weapon for defending anti-tank ditches. This flame device, called the "Adey-Martin Drain Pipe", was attached to the side of a carrier and tested by the Welsh Guards at Sandown Park. Further development work resulted in the prototype of what became the Ronson

3 in mortar assembled in front compartment of carrier.

Ronson projector in armoured housing.

Ronson flame-projecting equipment (prototype).

flame-throwing device. This was a pressure-operated equipment fitted to a Universal Carrier which featured two 60 gallon flame-fuel tanks attached to the outside rear of the vehicle, thereby allowing the carrier to retain its normal crew. The flame-gun was mounted on top of the front gunner's superstructure and the flame fuel was obtained through a flow pipe that ran along the left side of the vehicle to the rear fuel containers.

Due to certain limitations, which included the short range of the flame-projector (40 to 50 yds) and the vulnerability of the flame-fuel tanks outside the vehicle, this equipment was not accepted for service by the British War Office. The Canadian Army, however, maintained an interest in this vehicle and made arrangements for its production in Canada. Twenty of these Ronson flame devices were later sent from Canada to the Pacific area at the request of the US Marine Corps, where they were fitted in M3A1 Light Tanks. This equipment became known to the Americans as "Satan". In the meantime, further developments during 1941 and 1942 by the Petroleum Warfare Department had resulted in the first type of Wasp flame-thrower. Carriers fitted with Wasp equipment were designated as follows:

Wasp, Mk I (FT, Transportable, No 2, Mk I)
In this first version produced, the two flame-fuel tanks (40 and 60 gallons), pressure bottles, and connected equipment were stowed inside the carrier. The flame-projector, which was of a new design, had a range of 80 to 100 yds and was still mounted over the left front of the carrier. A crew of two was carried, the normal armament being discarded. An order for 1,000 was placed by the War Office in September 1942, production of the Wasp Mk I being completed by November 1943. Production was then switched to the Wasp Mk II, the Mk I being relegated to training purposes. Several Wasp Mk Is were equipped with swimming devices and used in floatation trials.

Wasp, Mk II.

Wasp Mk II (FT, Transportable, No 2, Mk II)
The first prototype of the Mk II was tested in August 1943 and proved to be much superior to the Mk I. The main difference as compared to the Mk I lay in the flame-projector which was of completely new design and was mounted in the machine gun housing of the carrier, making the vehicle less easily recognisable as a flame-throwing carrier. Though there was no great difference in range over the Mk I, the new flame-gun gave a better flaming performance and target effect was better since a larger proportion of the flame jet reached the target. The flame-gun also afforded increased ease of aiming, manipulation, and operation of the firing control. Elevation, traverse and depression were all increased and the gun mechanism was improved to give clean cut-off at the end of shots, thereby eliminating fire danger to the carrier. Some general re-design of the equipment reduced the weight and rendered vehicle maintenance much easier than with the Mk I. A crew of two was carried. The first formation to use the Wasp Mk II in

Wasp, Mk I.

Close-up of flame projector of the Wasp Mk II and IIC. Wasp, Mk IIC.

Carrier, Machine Gun, LP No 1.

Carrier, Machine Gun, LP No 1. Showing large stowage lockers on right side of vehicle.

action was the 53rd Division. On July 29 1944, six Wasp Mk II carriers of the 1st Highland Light Infantry were used in operations in the area of Eterville in support of D Company of the 2nd Monmouthshire Regiment.

Wasp Mk IIC (FT, Transportable, No 2, Mk IIC)
This was developed for the Canadian Army ("C" for "Canada") and appeared in August 1944, being used by the Canadian Army in the advance to Falaise. It differed from the Wasp Mk II in that only one flame fuel container of 75 gallons was carried, mounted outside the carrier at the rear of the vehicle, thereby leaving room in the vehicle for a third man with an LMG (Bren) or 2 in mortar. The flame-gun was of the type used in the Mk II and was mounted in the same position, ie, the machine gun housing. The Canadians had designed the Wasp IIC to obtain a combination of flame-thrower with the normal role of carrier and accepted the disadvantage of

the rear mounted fuel tank to attain this. The British Army had developed the Wasps Mks I and II for the role of flame-throwing only, not requiring the use of this vehicle in a carrier role while fitted with flame equipment. Experience in France proved the Canadians to be right and the Mk IIC version came to be universally preferred. After the production programme of the Mk II was completed in June 1944, all production was changed over to the Mk IIC. Some local conversions of the Mk II to Mk IIC standards were carried out in 21 Army Group utilising the 60 gallon tank of the Mk II equipment and mounting it at the rear. Plastic armour was also fitted to the fronts of Mk IIC Wasp Carriers in 21 Army Group for additional protection against German 7.92 mm AP shells and 20 mm fire.

By the beginning of 1945, the Wasp Mk IIC had replaced the Mk II in 21 Army Group. It became widely used and most infantry battalions were issued with six Wasps Mk IIC. By the end of the war the Mk IIC had been accepted as the standard British carrier-borne flame-thrower. Three Wasps were sent to Russia for evaluation in February 1945.

AUSTRALIAN AND NEW ZEALAND CARRIERS

Prior to the outbreak of the war in 1939, Australia, except for the building of a few experimental armoured cars in the late thirties, had had little experience of manufacturing armoured fighting vehicles relying on Britain to supply any requirements that were necessary. But, with the fall of France and the great loss of British equipment, Dominions' demands for military equipment could no longer be met, all production being required for home defence or for the army in the Middle East and exportable surplus would not be available for at least twelve months. Confronted with this situation, and with the prospect of a Japanese invasion, plans were made for the local production of armoured vehicles. With the decision to build carriers, it was decided to base them on

the British design, drawings of which were obtained from Britain. These were modified in detail to suit local manufacturing conditions, and a system was organised where various components were made by a number of engineering sub-contractors and assembled in Australian state-owned workshops, the power units being supplied from North America. Approximately 5,501 carriers were manufactured in Australia designated Carrier LP (LP for Local Pattern). Three basic models were built and various variants. New Zealand, like Australia, had no previous experience of manufacturing armoured vehicles, also relying on Britain to supply any requirements needed. Faced with the same situation as Australia, New Zealand also turned to local production.

The New Zealand State Railways workshops and the General Motors Co NZ were the builders in this case, and the working drawings and machine tools were supplied from Australia. Canada provided Ford engines and other mechanical components. The New Zealand-built vehicles were identical in virtually all respects to those built in Australia.

Carrier, Machine Gun, LP No 1
This vehicle was basically similar in appearance to the British Vickers Bren Carrier, but with minor differences. Large stowage lockers were fitted on the right side of the vehicle, clips were attached to the exterior of the superstructure for various accessories that included an axe, shovel, crank-handle and track tools. Wireless was carried by some vehicles. Armament consisted of a Vickers .303 in medium machine gun in the front gun housing, though this was sometimes replaced by a .55 in Boys anti-tank rifle or .303 in Bren LMG; the Bren LMG was also sometimes carried on an AA mount.

Brief details:
Crew 3 or 4
Weight 4 tons 5 cwt
Engine Ford V-8 95 bhp
Speed 30 mph

Universal Carrier, MG, LP No 2.

Universal Carrier, MG, LP, No 2

The major difference in this version was the adoption of the Universal welded superstructure and a change to the steering wheel instead of the lever steering controls of the first model. Large stowage lockers were carried at the rear of the vehicle which was fitted with 1938–39 Ford heavy duty commercial truck type rear axles.

Universal Carrier, MG, LP, No 2A

This variation was similar to the LP No 2 model, but had standard 1940 Ford heavy duty truck type rear axle.

Carrier, MG, Local Pattern, No 1 (New Zealand)

This type was identical to its Australian counterpart produced under this designation, but, in this case, the vehicles were built in mild steel due to the lack of armour plate. They were subsequently used for training only in New Zealand. Only 40 of these were made, starting in 1940.

Carrier, MG, Local Pattern, No 2 (New Zealand)

This type corresponded to its Australian counterpart in all respects and was the main production type. Approximately 500 of these vehicles were built, and were in use with the New Zealand Forces only.

THE WINDSOR AND T16 CARRIERS

Carrier, Windsor Mk I*

Introduced in 1943 (and at first known as the "Campbell Carrier"), the Windsor was built by the Ford Motor Company of Canada backed by the Canadian Department of Munitions and Supply. This vehicle was designed as a replacement for the Loyd Carrier as a towing vehicle. Incorporating 90 per cent of Loyd components, the design was based on the Universal Carrier but projected as a much larger and more powerful vehicle, the suspension system consisting of four road wheels and two return rollers either side. Armour was riveted bullet-proof steel plate throughout.

User trials of this vehicle proved so very satisfactory that it was proposed as an interim measure to replace all Loyd Carriers with the Windsor and serious consideration was given to developing the Windsor Carrier to

Carrier, Windsor. Mk I. Early production type*

undertake the functions of the Universal Carrier. Due to mechanical trouble experienced after production had begun, the vehicle was only in service in small numbers by the end of the war. The Windsor Carrier could be adapted for any of numerous special roles with necessary changes of the stowage arrangement. The different versions are described here.

4.2 in Mortar Platoon, Mortar Carrier

This vehicle had a crew of five, and carried 22 rounds of 4.2 in mortar ammunition on the trackguards in the rear compartment. It towed the mortar on a trailer.

4.2 in Mortar Platoon, Senior Commander's Vehicle

This had a crew of four men and carried 20 rounds of 4.2 in mortar ammunition. A Sten carbine and three rifles were carried in the rear compartment. A Bren LMG and ammunition was stowed in the front compartment. Provision was made for installation of a No 19 or No 22 W/T set in the right-hand rear compartment. A telephone loudspeaker control unit was stowed in a bin at the rear of the engine enclosure.

4.2 in Mortar Platoon, Junior Commander's Vehicle

This had a crew of two men and carried 48 rounds of 4.2 in mortar ammunition in the rear compartment plus a Bren LMG and ammunition in the front compartment

Carrier, Windsor. Mk I. Late production type.*

6 pdr Anti-Tank Gun Towing Carrier

This vehicle was used by some infantry battalions in 21 Army Group 1945, as a towing vehicle for A/T platoons instead of the Universal or Loyd. It had a crew of five men, and carried four boxes of 6 pdr ammunition and detachment stores in the rear compartment.

6 pdr Ammunition Carrier

A "limber" vehicle for the gun tower, it had a crew of two, carried four boxes of 6 pdr ammunition, plus main and auxiliary gun shields and 6 pdr gun spares and accessories in the rear compartment.

Basic specification for the Windsor Carrier was as follows:

Brief details:
Weight 9,350 lb (less stowage, crew, fuel)
Length 172$\frac{1}{4}$ in (overall) including tow hook
Width 83 in (overall)
Height 4 ft 9$\frac{1}{4}$ in
Armour 5–10 mm (front)   7 mm (sides and rear)
Engine Ford V-8 95 hp
Max speed 35 mph

Carrier, Universal, T16, Mk I

Designed in 1942, the T16 carrier was manufactured in the United States and was the result of experimental work carried out by the Ford Motor Company of America in an attempt to design a more satisfactory vehicle than the existing Universal and Loyd carriers.

While retaining the basic shape of the Universal, the principal changes in design provided for the use of the hand lever controlled differential steering system (the British Universal Carrier had wheel controlled steering), a Ford V-8 GAU Mercury engine, a re-designed and simplified welded hull structure, and refinement of the track and suspension, which now consisted of four road wheels (in units of two) and two return rollers either side. Three types of road wheel were used; up to the first 1,900 vehicles the spokes of the road wheel were straight, but after this they were curved. Solid disc wheels were also used.

Production of 30,000 vehicles for the British was authorised by an agreement between the British Tank

Carrier, Universal, T16, Mk I.

Mission to USA and the US Tank Committee, but only a limited number had been built and taken into British service by the end of the war. A few were used operationally by the Australians in the Far East. The T16 vehicles were intended to undertake the same roles as performed by the Universal Carrier, the transport of personnel and cargo, as tower for the 6 pdr anti-tank gun, and carrier for the 4.2 in mortar. When used in this role the base plate was carried on the bow and the barrel on the centre bulkhead.

Stowage arrangement for the British armament consisted of one PIAT, two Bren LMGs, one 2 in smoke mortar and two .303 in rifles. Provision for the installation of the British No 19 Wireless Set was also made.

Brief details:
Crew 4
Weight 10,500 lb
Length 12 ft 11$\frac{1}{8}$ in
Width 6 ft 11$\frac{1}{2}$ in
Height 5 ft 1 in
Armour $\frac{7}{32}$ in (hull front, upper) $\frac{9}{32}$ (front lower, sides and rear)
Max speed 30 mph

Carrier, Universal, T16E2, Mk II

This model was authorised to replace the T16 in production in 1945, basically similar to the T16, this vehicle was re-worked to improve stability and give better bogie

Carrier, Universal, T16, Mk I. Fitted with solid disc wheels.

Carrier, Universal, T16E2, Mk II.

The Oxford Carrier

Last in direct line of descent from the machine gun carriers of the 1930s was the Oxford Carrier which was also the last tracked carrier in British service before the adoption of the FV432 series of tracked APCs currently in use. The Oxford saw service in small numbers only and never completely supplanted the Universal Carrier. The last Oxford Carriers were not disposed of until 1963–64, many of those scrapped being virtually "as new" and never issued for service. The Oxford, and its derivative the Cambridge, are described below to complete the 30 year story of this type of vehicle.

Carrier, Tracked, CT20 (Carrier, Oxford, Mk I)

Though a few experimental types of tracked carrier were designed and pilot models built at the latter end of the war, the CT20 was the last of a series of vehicles that were descended from the Light Dragon Mk III of 1935. Designed to a specification intended to produce an improvement on the Loyd and Universal Carriers, the Oxford Carrier was designed to function as an all-purpose carrier. It was produced too late to be used operationally and production was limited. In the early post-war period, trials were carried out on prototypes for the roles of gun-tower for the 6 pdr and 17 pdr anti-tank guns, and as a carrier for the 3 in mortar.

The hull of the Oxford was of an open box-like welded construction embodying a double floor as protection against mine blast. The rear portion of the hull contained the covered engine, radiator, two fuel tanks and a Hydramatic transmission unit. The front portion of the hull contained the auxiliary gearbox, Cletrac steering unit, final drive, driver's seat and controls, and seating accommodation for the personnel. The driver was provided with episcope vision. The upper portion of the tracks and the track support rollers were covered by armoured skirt plates. Mounted above each track, and forming a part of the superstructure were dropsided stowage panniers. Suspension was of an improved Horstmann type with four bogie wheels coupled in two units with parallel coil springs. Hydraulic shock

loading. The front road wheel or bogie was moved back 6 in, the rear bogie was moved back 9 in and reversed, and the drive axle was moved back 8 in. This gave a ground contact length of 77 in as against the 71 in of the T16.

One experimental vehicle was based on the T16 and was known as "Tugboat". Projected in late 1944, this equipment was designed to combat anti-personnel mines ("S" mines, "Schu" mines, etc) which were laid with the normal German anti-tank mines. These anti-personnel mines were intended to prevent the mine clearing teams lifting the anti-tank mines.

The Tugboat consisted of a T16 with additional track and suspension units, sprockets, and idlers fitted to either side of the carrier in order to obtain minimum ground pressure. The vehicle was intended to tow a light mine roller across the minefield to detonate the anti-personnel mines without detonating the tank mines. The unstowed vehicle weighed 5 tons 3½ cwt and was experimental only.

Some T16 Carriers were retained by the British Army, and these remained in service until the 1950s. A number were used in foreign service and many were converted by an American firm as agricultural or commercial tractors. This conversion was known as the "SCAT". These vehicles had various types of super-structures constructed on the original hull.

Tugboat.

Above: *T16 in post-war service with the British Army.*

Below: *Carrier, Oxford, Mk I.*

Oxford Carrier towing 120 mm recoilless anti-tank gun.

absorbers were fitted between bogie wheel axles and the hull.

Brief details:

Weight 7 tons 17 cwt	**Armour basis** 20 mm
Length 14 ft 9 in	**Engine** Cadillac V-8 110 bhp liquid cooled
Width 7 ft 6½ in	**Max speed** 31.38 mph (road)
Height 5 ft 7 in	**Range** 126 miles

A number of experimental types were built to determine a possible replacement for the Oxford. The series is outlined here.

Carrier, Tracked, CT21-35R

This was a 35 cwt pay load carrier with Ford V-8 85 bhp engine at rear. Designed by Vivian Loyd Ltd, only one prototype was built.

Carrier, Tracked, CT22-35F

This was a 35 cwt pay load carrier, similar to CT21, but with the engine at front. One prototype only was built, also by Loyd.

Carrier, Tracked, CT23

Yet another of the test series, this was a 50 cwt pay load carrier with twin Ford V-8 engines at the rear.

Carrier, Tracked, CT24

Designed by Rolls-Royce, this vehicle had leaf spring suspension and had a hull similar to the Oxford's.

Carrier, Tracked, CT25

This vehicle was as for CT20 but fitted with a Rolls-Royce engine and Merritt-Brown gearbox and transmission.

Carrier, Tracked, CT26

This was a Vickers-Armstrong design of load carrier, based on A17 light tank chassis. Unladen weight was 10½ tons.

The Cambridge Carrier

Carrier, Tracked, FV 401 (Carrier, Cambridge)

This vehicle was designed by Rolls-Royce. It was projected in 1946 and the pilot model appeared in 1950. The Cambridge was of a box-like construction and was fitted with independent torsion bar suspension that was protected by armoured skirting. The engine, a Rolls-Royce B80, was located at the rear of the vehicle. The front crew compartment was fitted with four hinged armoured flaps that could be raised for extra protection; the driver was provided with episcope vision. The sides of the superstructure were fitted with stowage panniers. The vehicle was provided with a collapsible flotation

Carrier, Oxford as 3 in mortar carrier.

Carrier, Tracked. CT23.

Carrier, Tracked. CT24.

screen. Pilot models only built, and these were troop tested. No production followed.

Brief details:

Crew 7–8	**Width** 8 ft 5 in
Weight 9 tons 5 cwt	**Height** 5 ft 7 in
Length 15 ft 4 in	**Armour basis** 8–16 mm

Carrier, Armoured, OP No 4 (FV 402)

This was the FV 401 converted to an Armoured Observation Post. It was fitted with an armoured hatch over the crew compartment and carried the necessary wireless equipment.

Carrier, Tracked. CT26.

Above: *Carrier, Cambridge.*

Below: *The Cambridge carrier with flotation screen erected.*

Carrier, Armoured, O P No 4 (FV402).

PART SEVEN
THE UNIVERSAL CARRIER WITH MISCELLANEOUS DEVICES

Carriers were used in scores of specialised roles, many of them being no more than experimental.

Universal Carrier with Carpet Device, Mk I, Mk II and Mk III

The Carpet Device consisted of a reinforced Hessian carpet wound on a horizontal metal reel carried above the ground across the front of the vehicle by side arms attached to the vehicle. Its primary object was to enable the vehicle to cross barbed wire obstacles and to leave a pathway for following infantry and vehicles.

On meeting the obstacle, the weighted free end of the carpet was dropped on to the ground, whilst the vehicle ran forward. As soon as the tracks ran on to the free end, the carpet continued to unwind itself from the reel automatically, so that the carrier ran over it across the obstacle. After the carpet was laid the reel and framework was jettisoned. The three types were as follows:

Mk I (Infantry)—150 ft long × 11 ft 6 in wide. For general use with Carriers.

Mk II (Infantry)—150 ft long × 11 ft wide. For general use and operation from LCTs.

Mk III (LCM)—150 ft long × 8 ft wide. For operation from LCMs, hence the reduced width.

Universal Carrier with Carpet Device, Mk I, Mk II and Mk III.

Trials were first made with a carpet device fitted to a Cruiser Tank Mk I (A9) in March 1939 and by June 1940 a design had been prepared for a similar device for fitment to a Matilda II. Experiments during 1941 with a carpet device fitted to a Universal Carrier were concluded with satisfactory results, and by the end of the year a production order for 500 devices for fitment to the Universal Carrier was placed. In practice, however, these carpet devices were rarely used except on exercises.

Universal Carrier with Crossing Device

This experimental device for crossing swampy or sandy ground was tested in 1941. The device consisted of a carrier with a tubular frame mounted on its super-

Universal Carrier with Crossing Device.

structure, the frame extending and curving over the front of the vehicle. Carried on the frame was a number of linked wooden slats. The action of this device was similar to the carpet device. The carrier ran on to the free end of the wooden slats and the device automatically uncoiled as the carrier moved forward creating its own pathway.

Universal Carrier, Fitted with Demolition Device (Kid)

Evolved during 1944 for the demolition of small concrete walls by remote control, this experimental device consisted of a carrier with an adjustable metal frame mounted on the front of the vehicle. Attached to the frame was 600 lb of explosive. The frame of explosive was carried in a horizontal position until the obstacle was within range (200 yds). The frame was then moved to an upright position and the carrier was set on its course by the driver who jumped out when within effective range. The charge was automatically fired on contact and the carrier was considered expendable. The name "Kid" was a diminutive from the similar Goat device used with the Churchill tank.

Universal Carrier, fitted with Demolition Device (Kid).

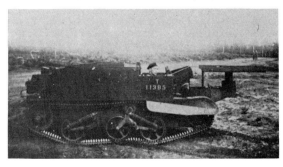

Towed Carrier, Fitted with Conger 2 in Mk I (Line Charge)

Evolved in January 1944 for mine clearance in assault, this device consisted of an engineless Universal Carrier containing a 5 in Rocket No 3 Mk I and projector, air bottles and a tank of explosive. Fitted to the rear of the carrier was a wooden box containing 330 yds of 2 in woven hose. The carrier was towed to the edge of the minefield and released by the towing vehicle (Sherman or Churchill AVRE). The empty hose was attached to the rocket which was fired from the projector across the minefield so that it lay extended across the field, one end of the hose still being connected to the carrier. The hose was then pumped full of explosive by compressed air. When sufficient explosive had been pumped into the hose the hose was disconnected from the carrier, which was removed. The hose was then fired by a delay pull igniter. The blast of the explosive hose detonated the mines in its area, thus creating a limited pathway through the minefield. The device saw limited service. Carriers were converted to Conger configuration by the well-known lock-making firm of Chubb & Sons Ltd, Wolverhampton.

Universal Carrier with Conger 1 in Device (Line Charge)

Evolved during March 1944, but not used in operations, this was a similar but smaller version of the Conger 2 in. Carried in the Universal Carrier Mk II, the vehicle was fully self-propelled, retaining its engine. The line-charge equipment could also be fitted to any carrier that had been modified to take Wasp FT equipment.

Wasp Flame-Thrower with MBSD

The multi-barrelled smoke-discharger (MBSD) consisted of a number of small tubes each holding a No 80 grenade (smoke) and a small electrically-fired propelling charge. The tubes could be fitted to the side or to the front of the vehicle and arranged radially so that the grenades were projected simultaneously to fall some 50 yds in front or to the flank of the vehicle in a fan-shaped arc of 120°. The discharger was operated by the vehicle commander by a control switch fitted inside the vehicle. An eight-barrelled type was also designed for the Wasp flame-thrower Universal Carrier to assist it to close on its target. This was used by the First Canadian Army.

Smoke Screening Apparatus for Mounting on Carrier

This was a low pressure spray apparatus consisting of two 5 gallon drums of charged CSAM with an air inlet feed, ejection pipe and manual air pipe. It was stowed in the rear stowage compartment behind the driver. It could be fitted by the crew and required no drilling. It was developed and put out for troop trials during the summer of 1943.

Carrier Ambulance

Used by the armoured units, this was the Universal Carrier modified with lengthened superstructure and open rear ends to allow a stretcher to be carried each side of the engine casing. Standard carriers were also used, the stretchers being laid across the hull top and a red cross flag being shown.

Universal Carrier, Anti-Aircraft

This was an experimental prototype of an anti-aircraft version of the Universal Carrier with a special all-round traverse turret fitted with two .303 Vickers "K" air-cooled machine guns and special sight. The turret was mounted over the gunner's compartment, the shape of

Towed Carrier, fitted with Conger 2 in Mk I (Line Charge).

Universal Carrier, Mk II in the role of ambulance.

Universal Carrier, Anti-Aircraft.

Rocket Assisted Egress on Universal Carrier.

which had been suitably altered. The driver's compartment on the right was also modified. Though tested in 1940–41, it was never placed in production.

Rocket Assisted Egress on Universal Carrier
Developed during 1946, this device was devised as a means whereby a bogged vehicle could be extracted from mud or water without the use of special recovery equipment. Two special 5 in rockets were fitted to each side of the carrier and when fired the thrust of the rockets propelled the carrier forward out of its bogged position.

Gutted Carrier; For Attachment to Tanks
The gutted carrier was the armoured shell of a normal OP or Universal Carrier riding on its suspension. From the carrier's interior all equipment had been removed, including the engine, steering, seats, etc. The gutted carrier was towed by means of two Hollebone draw-bars with an articulating eye. It could be towed at between 10 and 15 mph on the road and was capable of carrying two tons of stores. This conversion was the result of success achieved with armoured sledges used by AVREs but was developed too late for use during the war.

Universal Carrier with attachment for towing Artillery
In 1943 it was decided to fit the Stacey towing attachment to all new carriers coming off the production lines. The attachment was put into production because it was considered operationally essential that all carriers should be capable of towing the 6 pdr anti-tank gun short distances in an emergency. The attachment was also fitted to some earlier models of the Universal Carrier but not the Armoured OP vehicles.

Universal Carrier with Armoured Roof
The need for protection against aerial attack, considered necessary after experience in France in 1940, led to the fitting of light armoured roofs to some carriers of the Yeomanry Armoured Brigade in the United Kingdom during the invasion scare in the Summer of 1940. This idea was soon abandoned due to the crew's restricted vision and field of fire, and the added weight of the armoured roof which had an adverse effect on perform-

Carrier with PIAT Battery.

ance. The idea was devised by the Royal Gloucestershire Hussars who were equipped with carriers instead of tanks at a period of grave tank shortage.

Carrier with PIAT Battery
Improvised by the Canadians in 1944, this consisted of 14 PIAT (Projectile Infantry Anti-Tank) projectors mounted on a frame at the rear of the carrier in two series of seven. Each row could be fired simultaneously by means of a mechanical contrivance of steel rods attached to the firing triggers. A few vehicles so fitted were used in Europe in 1944–45.

Carrier, 2 pdr Equipped
This was the Canadian Universal Carrier Mk I* and Mk II* modified to permit the mounting of a 2 pdr gun with necessary ammunition and stowage. The ammunition was stowed along the sides and front of the division plate. The engine cover was redesigned to provide adequate clearance for the recoil of the gun. A total of 213 Carriers were converted to this role, and were used for training in Canada.

Carrier, 2 pdr, Tank Attack
Designed for an anti-tank role in 1942, this Australian version consisted of a 2 pdr anti-tank gun mounted on a lengthened and strengthened carrier chassis. The suspension was of the normal carrier type, but with a longer track (182 links as against 176). The engine was moved from the centre of the vehicle and placed on the left of the driver. The 2 pdr gun with shield was mounted on a turntable at the rear of the vehicle, the gun having a 360° traverse. Ammunition for the 2 pdr gun was carried in containers attached to the right side of the shield.

Brief details:
Crew 4 (three gunners and a driver)
Weight 5 tons approx.
Engine Ford V-8 95 bhp
Max speed 20 mph

Carrier, 2 pdr (Hydraulic Hoist)
This was another experimental self-propelled 2 pdr gun mounting, and consisted of a normal Australian LP, No 2 carrier with the gun fitted to a hydraulic hoist. This enabled the gun to be raised for firing with a 360° traverse and lowered when not in use. This equipment was situated behind the driver's compartment. When the gun was in the down position the barrel lay alongside the driver in a recess cut in the front plate.

Universal Carrier with armoured roof.

Carrier, 2 pdr (Hydraulic Hoist).

Carrier, 2 pdr (Hydraulic Hoist) in raised position.

Above: *Carrier, 2 pdr Tank Attack.*

Below: *Carrier, 2 pdr Equipped.*

Carrier, 3 in Mortar

Like the Carrier 2 pdr Tank Attack, this was a vehicle of modified design with a 3 in mortar on a turntable in the rear compartment, the engine being transferred to the left front of the carrier. The mortar could be fired from the carrier, the turntable allowing a 360° traverse. If required the mortar could be dismounted and fired from the ground. The mortar bombs were carried in racks arranged around the inside of the rear compartment. Also carried was a Bren LMG for AA defence. All details (aside from armament) were otherwise as for the 2 pdr Tank Attack.

The Universal Carrier, Local Pattern, was also used as a mortar carrier and in this case it consisted of the standard vehicle with the 3 in mortar mounted on (and fired from) the top of the engine compartment. It could also, of course, be dismounted and fired from the ground.

Praying Mantis

The "Praying Mantis" was designed and built by Messrs County Commercial Cars Ltd of Fleet, as a light armoured fighting vehicle, able to use natural cover to the best advantage. This feature was achieved by means of an armoured driving and fighting compartment that was able to be raised from the prone position to the horizontal until the gun mount was raised 12 ft above the ground.

The idea for this type of vehicle came about largely as a result of observations of a tank action during the first world war by a machine gun officer, Mr E. T. J. Tapp, who conceived the notion of developing a one-man armoured machine gun carrier with a low silhouette, but with a mechanical arrangement to enable the machine gun to be raised and fired from concealment. No more happened about the project until 1937 when the possi-

Carrier, 3 in Mortar.

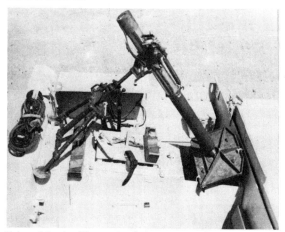

Universal Carrier, LP mounting the 3 in mortar on the engine compartment.

Praying Mantis in prone positon.

Praying Mantis in raised position.

bility of war again arose and Mr Tapp contacted General Sir E. Swinton, who showed great interest in the idea and urged immediate development of a prototype model. Work on the one-man machine was commenced late in 1937, trials taking place in October 1939, watched by General Martel, who as a result decided that a two-man version would be more suitable both from the consideration of morale and the control of the vehicle and its armament. Dimensions for this one-man vehicle were $4\frac{1}{2}$ ft wide and $2\frac{1}{2}$ ft high with the machine gun lowered.

Design work on a two-man machine was begun and completed by December 1940 but work on the construction of the vehicle was halted due to its low priority and the more urgent and heavy commitments for standard types of AFVs. In October 1941, interest was again revived and the original one-man machine was made ready for further demonstrations and tests. Resulting from this, in May 1942, a contract was placed with County Commercial Cars Ltd for the production of a two-man vehicle. This machine was built and tested over the period October to December 1943. Again due to now diminishing requirements for this type of vehicle, the Praying Mantis (called this because of its resemblance to the insect of that name) was returned to the manufacturer to be held in store. In June 1944 consideration was given to the use of this type of AFV for jungle warfare in the Far East but with no result and the idea was officially dropped.

For the construction of the Praying Mantis, standard Universal Carrier parts were used, the tracks being increased in length by having an extra 21 links inserted in each. A specially designed frame was mounted on the modified suspension with the engine and gearbox positioned in the rear. The armoured elevating compartment, which was rectangular in section, fitted horizontally into the frame. This was divided into three sections, the top section holding the driver and gunner who lay side by side. The lower two sections acted as legs; these passed back on either side of the engine to the trunnions and were hinged to the rear of the frame. These legs contained the hydraulic jacks and auxiliary suspension, and in addition had the driving controls passing down from the driver's compartment, through the hollow trunnions to the engine, gearbox and brakes.

The elevation of the fighting compartment could be controlled by either member of the crew from levers mounted on the floor of the compartment. Steering was applied from the steering wheel in the compartment through cables to a cam, track-warping mechanism then through cables to standard brakes. Gear changes were operated by Bowden cable control.

Fitted to the nose of the front section was the gun helmet which was maintained horizontally by means of compensating rods for any position of the fighting compartment. Directly above the gunner's head was a mounting holding two Bren guns which were inverted to allow the loading of the 30 or 100 round circular magazines from inside the compartment. The Bren guns could be fired singly or as a pair and were sighted by a periscope. The depression and elevation of the guns was 10°, but an additional 20° depression and elevation was available on the gun helmet, giving 30° in all. The helmet had a traverse of 360°. Armour was $\frac{1}{2}$ in thick and the laden weight 5 tons 2 cwt. Height fully elevated was 12 ft 4 in.

With suitable conditions carriers could be floated across water gaps with their full battle loads by either of two methods. Before flotation sets were fitted, certain preparations were necessary to waterproof the carrier. This applied more to the earlier marks of Universal Carrier than to the later, which were constructed with flotation in view, having a lighter welded hull. The different devices are described here.

Attachment, Carrier Flotation, Assault Boat, Mks II and III

A design for floating carriers on assault boats Mks II and III which showed great promise on its acceptance trials, this was perfected and made ready for production. The carrier was supported in the water by two assault boats; these were fixed with a set of equipment known as "Attachment Mk I, Carrier Flotation (Assault Boat)". The sets were adjustable and it was possible to use them with either mark of assault boat.

Essentially the set consisted of two light steel beams which spanned the carrier hull and were fixed to it by quick-action attachments. These beams projected a boat width either side of the carrier hull and had webbing straps, which held the boat up when travelling across country, and tubular members to transfer the load to the boat bottom when floating. The carrier propelled itself in the water by its tracks; the steering being assisted by a man with a paddle in each assault boat.

Attachment, Carrier Flotation, Kapok, Mks I and II

This equipment consisted of brackets for attaching kapok floats to the carrier to enable it to float. The Mk I flotation set consisted of eight special brackets for

Attachment, Carrier. Flotation, Assault Boat, Mk II and Mk III.

Attachment, Carrier, Flotation, Kapok Mk I and Mk II.

attaching nine kopak floats to the Carrier Universal Mk I.

The Mk II set consisted of ten brackets and was designed to fit all carriers except the T16, which required special rear brackets, and the AOP Mk III from which the charging engine at the rear had to be removed.

Improvised Floating Equipment
Various methods using local material to improve floating equipment for the carrier were used. These consisted of petrol tins, oil drums, timber and tarpaulins, etc. The success of the equipment depended on the ingenuity displayed in its construction and of the selection and positioning of the material.

Carrier fitted for Wading
In preparation for the Normandy landings, it was necessary to improve on the carriers' low wading height of only 2 ft 3 in. Carriers issued to the main assault divisions were therefore given heightened superstructure by the simple expedient of fitting on supplementary armour plates, these being held in place by metal bars or rods that were inserted through brackets that had been welded to the carrier and to extra plates.

All joints and orifices were sealed with waterproof compound and the engine was waterproofed. The wading height was now brought up to approximately 5 ft so that the carriers could go ashore from landing craft with a much reduced risk of swamping. The driver had to be conned by the commander for this operation but once ashore the front supplementary plate was removed to give normal view. This conversion was also used in other theatres of war.

Carrier fitted with Cable Laying Equipment
Some carriers were fitted with Cable Laying Equipment, the mechanical cable layer being mounted on the engine compartment, and the spare cable drums stowed at the rear of the vehicle. One carrier adapted for cable laying was used to lay cable across the Irrawady river during the bridgehead battle in January 1945. The vehicle was fitted with empty petrol drums to achieve buoyancy. These vehicles were used by the Royal Signals.

Carrier with Assault Bridge
This improvised device was initiated in the UK in 1943 as a method of transporting anti-tank equipment quickly across small rivers or streams. The carrier was water-

Improvised Flotation Equipment.

Carrier fitted for Wading.

Carrier with Assault Bridge.

Left: *Carrier fitted with Cable Laying Equipment.*

proofed and trackway from "Raft Anti-Tank Gun" equipment was used. Two wooden spars were lashed to the top of the hull of the carrier and on top of the spars were positioned two sections of trackway. A further two sections of trackway were hinged to their front ends and supported at an angle of 45° by two cables attached to the rear of the vehicle. The carrier was driven into the river or stream and the raised trackway lowered.

Carrier, Mine Clearing

This was a post-war device used for the clearing of mines on British beaches and consisted of a carrier mounting a powerful water jet in the front superstructure, protected by armour shield. The water supply was obtained through hose pipes connected to reservoirs placed at a safe distance. The direction of the jet was controlled by an operator who was linked by phone to the water supply.

Carrier, 25 mm Hotchkiss SP

A local conversion of the carrier to a self-propelled mount for the French 25 mm Hotchkiss anti-tank gun, carried out by the French forces in Syria.

Carrier, with Recoilless A/Tk Gun

This was a post-war conversion of the Universal Carrier to a light self-propelled gun.

A 106 mm recoilless anti-tank gun was mounted above the engine with the protruding front barrel supported by stays. The gun was enclosed by a superstructure made of canvas and tubular rods, the front machine gun housing being blanked off.

Carrier, Crash Rescue

This vehicle was used by the Ministry of Supply in the late 1950s for crash rescue work at one of its establishments.

British Scout Carrier in use with the German Army in Russia as troop carrier.

The vehicle carried a wide range of equipment that included VHF two-way radio communication, single stretcher, spotlight, rescue equipment, and a small motor on the front for making foam in case of fire.

CARRIERS IN ENEMY SERVICE, 1940–1945

A number of carriers captured at Dunkirk or during the fighting in the Western Desert were taken into service by the Germans and Italians for their own use, many being altered for specific roles. The Japanese also captured a few carriers and used them against their former owners.

German

Official German designation of the Bren Universal Carrier as listed in the *Captured Foreign Equipment* manual (*Fremden Geräts, Kraftfahrzeuge*) was:

Gepanzerter MG Trager Br 731 (e) (gp MG Tr Br 731 (e)

The same designation with the number 732 was applied

Carrier, Mine Clearing.

Carrier, 25 mm Hotchkiss SP.

Carrier, with Recoilless A/Tk Gun.

Carrier, Crash Rescue.

to the Scout Carrier. There was no differentiation between the Bren or Universal Carrier, both types being called "Bren Carrier" in German.

Mun Schl Bren (e) (Munition Schlepper)
This was the British carrier (of any type) adapted as an ammunition or supply tractor. Many were used by the German occupation forces in France from 1940 on.

Mun Schl Bren fuer MG 08 (e)
This version had a Maxim machine gun Model '08 fitted on a pedestal mount in the front compartment. It was mainly used for airfield defence by the Luftwaffe.

Le Felad Tr Bren (e)
This was a Bren or Universal Carrier converted to a remote control explosive carrier. The superstructure was removed and the hull covered over, the interior being packed with explosives and fitted with radio control gear.

Schneeschaufel auf Bren (e)
Carrier converted to Snow Plough with superstructure removed and a small plough attached to the front of the vehicle. It was used by the German Army, and also by the Luftwaffe for clearing runways.

3.7 cm Pak auf Fahrgestall Bren (e)
This was the conversion of the carrier to a self-propelled mount for the 3.7 cm anti-tank gun. Only a few were so converted. The gun and shield were mounted on the engine behind the front compartment.

Panzerjaeger, Bren
The German Army modified a number of captured Universal Carriers in the latter part of the war as Tank Hunters. These were equipped with Panzerfaust (a hand weapon that fired a large hollow charge anti-tank bomb by percussion from a tube that contained the propellent charge) and Raketen Panzerbuches (Rocket Launchers – the German equivalent of the American Bazooka). These vehicles were formed into sections to create fast moving tank hunting teams.

Mun Schl Bren fuer MG 08(e).

Schneeschaufel auf Bren(e).

Panzerjaeger, Bren.

Italian

Carriers captured by the Italians in the Western Desert were frequently used against their former owners, the only changes to the carrier being the fitting of Italian weapons.

Cingoletta Fiat 2800

Built by the Italian firm of Fiat in 1942, this vehicle was a direct copy of the Universal Carrier. The superstructure, suspension and tracks were identical to its British counterpart, the armour thickness on the Italian version being slightly thicker. The Italian-built vehicle weighed 4.76 tons and carried a crew of two. It was powered with a 66.5 bhp engine, and attained a speed of 60 km per hour. Armament carried was a Breda 38 machine gun fitted in a ball mount in the front machine gun housing. It was not accepted by the Italian Army.

Japanese

A few carriers were captured by the Japanese at Singapore, Hong Kong, and elsewhere in 1941–42. One or two of these are known to have been converted to rudimentary light tanks by plating over the superstructure. A crude turret was built centrally towards the rear with a hinged raised cupola and a machine gun. Driver and front gunner occupied their usual positions. These vehicles were used in action; others, unconverted, were used as supply carriers.

PART EIGHT

THE LOYD CARRIER

The Loyd Carrier was introduced in 1940, built by the firm of Vivian Loyd and Co Ltd and various motor companies including Dennis, Wolseley, and the Ford Motor Company of Canada, Captain V. Loyd having left the firm of Vickers to establish his own concern after the death of his partner, Sir John Carden, in an air crash during 1935. Designed for a variety of roles which included the carriage of weapons ranging from machine guns to anti-tank guns and the transport of troops and stores, the chassis was composed largely of Ford commercial vehicle parts to assure cheap and rapid production. Unfortunately, at the time of its appearance in 1939–40, the demand for light tracked carriers was limited. Initially the Loyd Carrier was only used by the British Army as a troop carrier due to its advantage of having accommodation for eight men. However, it was later adopted as a towing vehicle and proved very popular. It was also developed to fulfil other ancillary roles, such as cable laying, and for carrying slave batteries. Its major importance, however, arose from the sudden urgent and larger requirements for mobile anti-tank guns, particularly in the Western Desert fighting.

Due to the demand for the use of the Loyd as a towing vehicle for the 2 pdr and (later) 6 pdr gun a requirement arose for improved load capacity and tractive ability, both of which were considered inadequate for a gun tower. Work was undertaken, therefore, to develop several improved models during 1943, but due to the continued demand for the Loyd as a 6 pdr gun tractor in quantity, the mechanical weakness of this vehicle was accepted and no modifications were allowed to be incorporated that would slow or delay production of the machine.

The towing requirement for which the Loyd was chosen could well have been undertaken by the Universal Carrier, however, and the Stacey towing attachment was

3.7 cm Pak auf Fahrgestall Bren(e).

Captured Universal Carrier in service with the Italian Army in the Western Desert.

Cingoletta Fiat 2800.

Japanese conversion of British carrier to light tank.

fitted to all Universal Carriers (except the OP version) built in 1943, enabling this vehicle to tow the 6 pdr anti-tank gun in an emergency over short distances. Nonetheless, the Loyd Carrier was preferred by the troops because its steering and handling were not as complicated as in the Universal. The limitation of carriers to these two basic types considerably reduced production problems, especially as there were a number of components common to both vehicles. Production of the Loyd Carrier was also undertaken by the Ford Motor Co of Canada.

The basic carrier was of an open type construction, with the engine fitted at the rear of the vehicle, and the drive taken forward to a front final driving axle. The front axle was fitted with driving sprockets to engage the track. Steering was effected by two steering levers, fitted in front of the driver's seat, operating on the brakes. Armour plate could be fitted to suit the various roles of the vehicle.

The following is an outline of the various Loyd types and special purpose conversions. The official (and often cumbersome) designation is given in each case.

Carrier, Tracked, Personnel Carrying, No 1, Mk I
This was the basic vehicle for the troop carrying role. It was characterised by the exposed front axle and differential housing. Hortsmann-type suspension was standard with four bogie wheels and two return rollers per side. The vehicle was fitted with Bendix brakes and had a British-built engine.

Brief details:	
Weight 4 tons	**Height** 4 ft 8¼ in (minus hood)
Crew 2 plus 8 men	7½ ft (with hood in position)
Length 13 ft 7 in	**Armour** mild steel
Width 6 ft 9½ in	**Engine** Ford V-8 85 bhp
	Max speed 30 mph (road)

Carrier, Tracked, Personnel Carrying, No 2, Mk I
Similar to the Loyd TPC No 1, Mk I, this version was fitted with a re-worked American-built Ford V-8, 95 bhp engine, EGAE.

Carrier, Tracked, Personnel Carrying, No 2A, Mk I
This was similar to the Loyd TPC No 1, Mk I but was fitted with a re-worked American-built Ford V-8, 90 bhp engine, EGAEA.

Carrier, Tracked, Personnel Carrying, No 3, Mk I
Similar in all respects to the TPC No 1, Mk I, but built in Canada.

Carrier, Tracked, Personnel Carrying, No 1, Mk II
Basically Carrier, TPC, Mk I, but fitted with Girling brakes.

Carrier, Tracked, Personnel Carrying, No 2, Mk II
As for TPC No 1, Mk II, but with re-worked American-built Ford V-8, 90 bhp engine, EGAE.

Carrier, Tracked, Personnel Carrying, No 2A, Mk II
As for TPC No 1, Mk II, but with re-worked American-built Ford V-8, 90 bhp engine, EGAEA.

Carrier, Tracked, Personnel Carrying, No 3, Mk II
This vehicle was as for TPC No 1, Mk II, but Canadian-built.

Carrier, Tracked, Starting and Charging, No 1, Mk I
The starting up of tank engines from cold, and the necessity to maintain a wireless watch proved to be a great drain on tank batteries, so the Loyd carrier was equipped with a Battery Charging Unit, and other equipment to act as a Slave Unit to start vehicles unable to start under their own power and to charge or replace AFV batteries. This Slave vehicle was basically Carrier, TPC, No 1, Mk II, fitted with the necessary equipment.

Carrier, Tracked, Starting and Charging, No 2, Mk I
As for Carrier, TS and C, No 1, Mk I, but with re-worked American-built Ford V-8, 90 bhp engine, EGAE.

Carrier, Tracked, Starting and Charging, No 2A, Mk I
As for Carrier, TS and C, No 1, Mk I, but with re-worked American-built Ford V-8, 90 bhp engine, EGAEA.

Carrier, Tracked, Starting and Charging, No 3, Mk I
This was as for Carrier, TS and C, No 1, Mk I, but Canadian-built.

Carrier, Tracked, Towing, No 1, Mk I
With the demand for mobile anti-tank guns due to the situation in the Western Desert, the Loyd Carrier was adapted to tow the 2 pdr and later the 6 pdr anti-tank guns, with the necessary stowage arrangements for gun crew, ammunition and gun accessories.

Carrier, Tracked, Towing, No 1, Mk I was basically

The Loyd Carrier.

Carrier, Tracked, Personnel Carrying, No 1, Mk I.

Carrier, Tracked, Starting and Charging, No 1, Mk I.

Carrier, Tracked, Towing, No 1, Mk II. 6 pdr gun.

Carrier, Tracked, Towing, No 1, Mk II. 4.2 in mortar.

Carrier, Tracked, Mechanical Cable Layer, Mk I.

Carrier, TCP, Mk II adapted for the 2 pdr anti-tank gun role.

Carrier, Tracked, Towing, No 2, Mk I
Basically Carrier, TPC, No 2, Mk I adapted for the 2 pdr anti-tank gun role.

Carrier, Tracked, Towing, No 2A, Mk I
Basically Carrier, TPC, No 2A, Mk I adapted for the 2 pdr anti-tank gun role.

Carrier, Tracked, Towing, No 3, Mk I
This was basically Carrier, TCP, No 3, Mk I adapted for the 2 pdr anti-tank gun role.

Carrier, Tracked, Towing, No 1, Mk II
This was basically Carrier, TPC, No 1, Mk II adapted for towing a 6 pdr anti-tank gun or 4.2 in mortar and equipment.

Carrier, Tracked, Towing, No 2, Mk II
Basically Carrier, TPC No 2, Mk II adapted for towing the 6 pdr anti-tank gun or 4.2 in mortar and equipment.

Carrier, Tracked, Towing, No 2A, Mk II
This was basically Carrier, TCP, No 2A, Mk II adapted for towing the 6 pdr anti-tank gun or 4.2 in mortar and equipment.

Carrier, Tracked, Towing, No 3, Mk II
This version was as for Carrier, TCP, No 3, Mk II but

adapted for the 6 pdr anti-tank gun or 4.2 in mortar towing roles.

Carrier, Tracked, Towing, No 1Z, Mk II
This vehicle was similar to Carrier, TT, No 1, Mk II, but with an American Ford type axle.

Carrier, Tracked, Towing, No 2Z, Mk II
As for Carrier, TT, No 2, Mk II, but fitted with an American Ford type axle.

Carrier, Tracked, Towing, No 2AZ, Mk II
This was as for Carrier, TT, No 2A, Mk II, but was fitted with an American Ford type axle.

Carrier, Tracked, Towing, No 3Z, Mk II
Again this vehicle was similar to Carrier, TT, No 3, Mk II, but was fitted with an American Ford type axle.

Carrier, Tracked, Mechanical Cable Layer, Mk I
This vehicle was based on the Carrier, TPC, No 1, Mk II, but had modifications to the superstructure for the fitment of cable laying stores, a ladder and poles being carried in brackets on either side. Mounted on the front of the vehicle were three drums of cable and carried in the centre of the vehicle was the mechanical cable laying machine which paid out telephone wires to the rear as the vehicle moved forward. This vehicle was widely used by the Royal Signals and to some extent by other arms like the artillery.

E

Carrier, Loyd AA.

Carrier, Loyd, Self-Propelled Gun, First version.

Carrier, Loyd AA

This was an experimental anti-aircraft conversion and featured a centrally mounted traversing platform with an armoured covered seat for the gunner and the quad Bren LMG with associated sighting equipment. An armoured box was also fitted for the driver. It was produced in 1942–43.

Carrier, Loyd, Self-Propelled Gun

The project for using the Loyd Carrier as a self-propelled mount for the 2 pdr anti-tank gun was projected in late 1940 and developed in 1941. Based on Carrier, TCP, Mks I and II, three versions of this equipment were built in small numbers and tested. Due to mechanical and other faults, modifications were found necessary so production on a large scale never began, the project being abandoned in December 1942 as the result of the introduction of more powerful anti-tank weapons.

In the first version, the 2 pdr gun was mounted in the front compartment, left of the driver, with the gun barrel protruding through an opening that had been cut in the front superstructure.

Carrier, Loyd, Self-Propelled Gun, Second version.

In the second version, the 2 pdr gun was fitted with a front shield, and was mounted centrally on the vehicle. This position achieved an all-round traverse but gave a high silhouette and limited protection to the gun crew.

For the third model, to effect a lower silhouette, the gun, fitted with a three-sided shield, was mounted at the rear of the vehicle, the engine being moved forward. A traverse of 200° was achieved for the gun.

Carrier, Loyd, Self-Propelled Gun, Third version.

Carrier, Loyd, 25 pdr Gun/How

This was an experimental conversion, the 25 pdr gun being mounted in the front of the carrier, from which the front superstructure had been removed.

Bridge, SP, Tracked

Projected in early 1940, this experimental vehicle was built and tested in 1941. It was 30 ft long and based on Loyd Carrier components and was intended to serve as a tracked mobile bridge for tanks up to 25 tons and for light wheeled vehicles.

Carrier, Loyd, Mobile Welding Plant

An experimental conversion of the Loyd Carrier, to carry welding equipment. The top superstructure was removed and the generating plant fitted across the centre of the vehicle. A canopy was erected for the driver and fitter.

CATI (Canon Anti Tank d'Infanterie)

Adopted by the Belgian Army after the war, the Loyd was converted into a self-propelled mount for the 90 mm gun.

PART NINE
WHEELED, HALF-TRACK AND KANGAROO CARRIERS

Carrier, Guy, Universal, Wheeled

In November 1939 an order was placed with Guy Motors Ltd for a wheeled carrier based on the Guy armoured car. This experimental vehicle, tested in June 1940, consisted of an open box type body of mild steel, and was very similar in design to the tracked carrier, with the fighting compartment in the front having the normal LMG housing. Various Universal Carrier fittings were attached to the superstructure and the engine was situated at the rear in an armoured box. There was one prototype only, and the type was not taken into service.

Carrier, Wheeled, Indian Pattern

Designed to function in the same role as the Universal Carrier, this series of vehicles was produced in India during 1940–44 and they were based on Ford 4 × 4 chassis that were manufactured by the Ford Motor Company of Canada and shipped to India where they

Carrier, Loyd, 25 pdr Gun/Howitzer.

Carrier, Loyd. Mobile Welding Plant.

Carrier, Guy, Universal, Wheeled.

Carrier, Wheeled, Indian Pattern. Mk I.

were assembled and armoured.

Various marks and sub-marks of this carrier existed and they were used in the Middle East, Italy, and the Far East.

Basically the Indian Pattern Carrier was an open top 4 × 4 vehicle with the engine at the rear and with the driver at the front right-hand side behind flat sloping armour; a hinged hatch was provided to the left of the driver to mount a LMG or Boys anti-tank rifle.

Brief details:
Crew 3–4
Weight 5 tons 6 cwt (approx)
Engine Ford V-8 95 hp

A wireless set could be fitted and there were variants fitted with a turret. A few of these wheeled carriers were used by the Commonwealth Brigade in Korea, 1950–53.

Truck, Armoured, 15 cwt, 4 × 4 (G.M. C15TA)

Produced in Canada during 1944, and intended to replace the M3AI Scout Car and 15 cwt half-track as personnel carriers in the Canadian Army. This was an open top wheeled vehicle with armoured cab, sides and rear. In the role of a personnel carrier, this vehicle could carry eight men including the driver, and their equipment. The seats and the height of the vehicle sides were arranged to permit shooting over the hull sides. This vehicle with modifications, could also be converted as an Armoured Ambulance or Armoured Load Carrier.

CAPLAD

Designed to replace the various types of armoured wheeled vehicles operating in specialised roles, the

Carrier, Wheeled. Indian Pattern. Mk IIA.

CAPLAD was a rear-engined all-purpose armoured vehicle designed to function, when fitted with the appropriate equipment, in the various roles of Command, Armoured Personnel, Light Aid Detachment, Ambulance or Demolition vehicles. The name "CAPLAD" being derived from the initials of its proposed functions. Prototype machines were developed and tested during 1943 and 1944 and a similar pilot model was built concurrently in Canada, the hull being based on the UK design but with the chassis designed in Canada. After various trials it was decided that the CAPLAD, as an armoured personnel carrier, had not sufficient space to accommodate the increased requirements for this role. Considerable interest, however, was shown in the vehicle operating in the role of a Command vehicle,

Truck, Armoured, 15 cwt, 4 × 4 (G.M. C15TA).

CAPLAD (British version).

CAPLAD (Canadian version).

Truck, 15 cwt, 4 × 4 Armoured Personnel.

but due to the fact that this vehicle would have to be produced in Canada, and that there was only a limited requirement, there being no demand for the vehicle in the personnel role, this did not justify production capacity being switched over to the manufacture of these vehicles, and so the CAPLAD project was shelved.

Truck, 15 cwt, 4 × 4, Armoured Personnel

Standardised in June 1939 as the M3AI Scout Car for the US Army, this vehicle was used in limited numbers by the British Army as an armoured personnel carrier. With modifications it was also adapted by the British Army to the roles of armoured ambulance, signals vehicle and 6 pdr gun tractor. As an APC, seats were provided in the driver's compartment for the driver and commander, and in the personnel compartment for six additional passengers. The vehicle's armament consisted of a cal .50 and a cal .30 machine gun mounted on a skate rail which encircled the interior of the body, permitting the gunners to fire in any direction.

Truck, 15 cwt, Half-Tracked, Personnel

This designation was applied to various US half-tracked vehicles taken into service with the British Army. These consisted of Carrier, Personnel, Half-Tracked, M5AI. Car, Half-Tracked, M9AI and the M14 Multiple Gun Motor Carriage. The M14 originally mounted twin cal .50 machine guns on a high angle mount for anti-aircraft defence, but due to the Allied

Truck, 15 cwt, Half-Tracked, Personnel.

supremacy of the air, the need for this type of weapon was no longer required and the M14 GMC was stripped of its armament and converted to General Service or Personnel Carrier. In the role of personnel carriers, these vehicles carried 12 infantrymen and a driver. They were also used as weapon carriers for the Vickers machine gun or 3 in mortar teams, tractors for the 6 pdr and 17 pdr anti-tank guns or as signal or ambulance vehicles.

Limited numbers of these vehicles remained in service with the British Army during the post-war period, well into the 1960s, being used as Cargo or

Ford, 3 ton 4 × 4, Armoured Lorry. (J. J. Clarke MM)

Bedford 3 ton 4 × 4 Armoured Lorry. (*Soldier* Magazine)

Personnel Carriers, Wireless or Command Vehicles, Carrier for Radar Equipment for the RA (CT Radar, FA, No 1) and as a AFV repair vehicle, winch-equipped vehicles being adapted for this role, having a folding "A" frame or jib mounted on the front.

Ford, 3 ton 4 × 4, Armoured Lorry

Used in Malaya by the British Forces during the Emergency, these vehicles were created to overcome the shortage of armoured personnel carriers urgently required for the transportation of troops through the jungle terrain of this country. Converted at the Singapore Base Workshops, the vehicles, Canadian 3 ton 4 × 4 Fords that were in general use, were fitted with armoured bodies that were made locally. They were replaced during 1954 by the British 3 ton Bedford lorries that had been similarly armoured.

Truck, 1 ton, Armoured 4 × 4, Humber (FV 1611)

This is an armoured version of the standard 1 ton Humber truck designed as a load or personnel carrier for infantry, armoured and other front line units. It was developed during the mid-1950s to supplement the Saracen APC then coming into service. No longer in

Truck, 1 ton, Armoured 4 × 4 Humber (FV1611).

production, the FV 1611 has been used with suitable modifications in a number of roles; Armoured Radio Truck, FV 1612, Armoured Ambulance FV 1613, towing and control vehicle for Green Archer mortar locating radar, and as the basis for the FV 1620 Hornet Malkara missile launcher. The Humber 1 tonner was being phased out of service in the late 1960s but the Northern Ireland emergency situation of 1968–72 gave it a new lease of life where it proved most useful for patrol and escort work in civil disturbances. The vehicle was popularly known as the "Pig". Local modifications in Northern Ireland included stoneguard mesh over all apertures, and a metal or perspex cupola above the driver's cab. In patrol and riot conditions the "Pig" proved a very useful vehicle in a true armoured personnel carrier role.

Kangaroos (Armoured Personnel Carriers)
Ram Kangaroo

Developed by the Canadian Army for carrying troops forward under fire, the Ram Kangaroo was first used in the assault on Boulogne in 1944, and consisted of a turretless Ram tank with suitable alterations to the

FV1620. Hornet, Malkara missile launcher.

Ram Kangaroo.

Priest Kangaroo.

interior stowage, producing a vehicle capable of carrying a section of eight infantrymen and their equipment. As this vehicle had proved so successful it was decided to convert a British regiment for the same role, an armoured brigade workshop converting 120 Ram tanks including major alterations to stowage and the fitting of wireless sets in one month. Similar conversions were made to the Priest, an American self-propelled 105 mm howitzer and the Sherman III.

Priest Kangaroo

The conversion of the Priest to the APC role involved the removal of the 105 mm howitzer and mantlet and the blanking off of the gap left by this removal; the ammunition bins were also removed and the wireless set reposi-

Churchill Kangaroo.

tioned. The armour sides were raised to the level of the front superstructure and facilities were provided for the mounting and dismounting of the personnel. The vehicle so equipped carried 12 infantrymen and a crew of two.

Sherman Kangaroo

This again involved the removal of the main armament and turret, alteration of interior stowage, the fitting of a wireless set and the provision for carrying a crew of two and ten infantrymen. A similar conversion was made with the Centaur tank, but this last converted vehicle did not see action.

Badger Flame-Thrower

This was another Canadian development, and consisted of fitting a Wasp Mk II flame-throwing unit to a Ram Kangaroo, to achieve better armour protection, cross-country performance and manoeuvrability than the Universal carrier. The Wasp gun replaced the bow machine gun, and comprised its only armament. Two fuel tanks (the 40 gal and 60 gal tanks of the Wasp Mk II) and the pressure bottles were fitted inside the vehicle. These vehicles became available in February 1945 and were used successfully by the Lake Superior Regiment (Motorised).

Churchill Kangaroo (FV 3904)

This was a post-war conversion of the Churchill Mk VII to an armoured personnel carrier of the Kangaroo type. The turret and main armament were removed and the interior of the vehicle adapted to accommodate a section of infantry with full equipment. Wireless equipment was installed and the front machine gun retained.

PART TEN
THE SARACEN AND VARIANTS

Armoured Carrier, 6 × 6 Personnel, Saracen (FV 603)

Produced by Alvis Limited to a War Office specification,

Armoured Carrier, 6 × 6 Personnel, Saracen.

this six-wheeled drive armoured personnel carrier entered service during 1952, its development and production being hastened by the need for a vehicle for counter-insurgency in Malaya. It was based on the Alvis Saladin armoured car using the same chassis and mechanical units, except that the layout was reversed to put the engine at the front. The Saracen was used as a carrier for personnel in armoured and armoured car regiments and in divisional engineer units. The Saracen is capable of quick conversion to the role of Fitters' Vehicle, Command Vehicle, Infantry Command Post, Signals Vehicle, Cargo Vehicle, Armoured Ambulance or Navigational Vehicle by the removal of the interior fittings and the installation of the appropriate equipment; entry is by double rear doors. Also developed on the FV 603 chassis was a Regimental Command Vehicle and a Gun Position Officer's Vehicle.

As a Personnel Carrier, the vehicle carries 12 men, including driver and commander, or seven men and a quantity of RE stores. The Saracen is sealed for wading to a depth of 3 ft 6 in, later vehicles to a deeper depth with special equipment. The armoured body protects the enclosed personnel against shell splinters, small arms fire, nuclear blast and heat flash. A small turret with 360° hand traverse mounts a .30 Browning machine gun for use against ground targets and a hatch in the rear of the roof enables a Bren light machine gun on a ring mount to be operated against aircraft. A tripod is carried on the vehicle to enable the .30 machine gun to be used for dismounted action. Three smoke dischargers are mounted on the front of each wing. The sides of the vehicle are fitted with hinged ports for use of the personnel weapons.

Brief details:

Weight 10 tons   **Width** 8 ft 3 in
Length 15 ft 11 in   **Height** 8 ft
Engine B80 Mk 3A 8 cylinder petrol
Speed 35 mph (average road) 20 mph (cross country)
Range of action 250 miles (an average maximum speed)

Three models of the Saracen APC existed for British military service.

Saracen, Mk I (FV 603A)
Original production model.

Saracen, Mk II (FV 603B)
Redesigned turret and modifications.

Saracen, (FV 603C)
This vehicle incorporates reverse flow cooling and air conditioning for operating in the Middle East.

Desert Saracen
This was a private venture, open topped variant offered for export sale to the Middle East powers. It was not used by the British.

Armoured Carrier, 6 × 6 Regimental Command (FV 604A)
This version of the Saracen was developed by the RAC and Signals as a Regimental Command Vehicle. Based on the FV 603, this vehicle was modified internally for fitting a combination of radio sets suitable for regimental commanders; it has modified seating accommodation for driver, commander, two radio commanders and

Saracen (FV603C).

Saracen, Mk II (FV603B).

Armoured Carrier, 6 × 6 Regimental Command (FV 604A).

Armoured Carrier, 6 × 6 Command GPO/CPO (FV 610A).

three staff officers. Other interior fittings include desks and mapboards. The turret is removed and replaced by a hatch with a ring mount for a light machine gun. External fittings include extra batteries and an auxiliary charging plant. A canvas penthouse tent can be erected to enable a Command Post to be established when the vehicle is stationary.

Armoured Carrier,
6 × 6 Command GPO/CPO (FV 610A)

Again basically the same vehicle as the Saracen APC, this version was originally designed as a Royal Artillery GPO/CPO Vehicle, but has since been adapted for use as a Command Post for Regimental/Brigade/Division Headquarters. To enable the occupants to work for long periods, the height was increased to permit standing and the body was widened to allow the installation of additional radio sets and equipment. Additional accommodation is provided by two canvas shelters which are stowed on the exterior of the hull when not in use.

All the variants of the Saracen family remained in service in 1972, though the FV 432 series vehicles had supplanted it to some extent, especially in infantry service.

Armoured Carrier, 6 × 6 Surveillance Radar (Robert).

Armoured Carrier, 6 × 6 Surveillance Radar ("Robert")

An experimental version of FV 610 mounting radar equipment. It was known as "Robert". It saw service only in prototype form for troop trials in the early 1960s.

Saracen with Swingfire Weapon System

Projected as a private venture, this was the Saracen Mk 2 adapted to carry two Swingfire anti-tank missiles, mounted either side of the hull, the interior of the vehicle being modified for stowage of six spare missiles. A retractable periscope is fitted behind the turret to allow the commander to control the fire and flight of the missiles.

PART ELEVEN
THE FV 430 AND SPARTAN

Armoured Personnel Carrier, FV 430 Series

The FV 430 tracked carrier series was developed to provide armoured mobility for personnel of the fighting arms under conditions of conventional or nuclear warfare. Designed at the Fighting Vehicles Research and Development Establishment, the requirements for this tracked carrier were first proposed in 1958 and the first prototype was delivered for trials in February 1961. Production was begun in 1962 by John Sankey and Sons Ltd of Smethwick. Considerable study of contemporary foreign designs was made during the development period. An American M59 APC was purchased for trials as was the Anglo-German HS 30. The resulting vehicle owed something of its shape and layout to the American M59 and M113 APCs (resembling the latter quite closely) but the influence of the Cambridge Carrier is also apparent. The basic model of the FV 430 series is the FV 432 APC; this vehicle carries a complement of 12 men, consisting of a driver, commander and ten infantrymen (ie, a complete rifle section – three vehicles carry a complete platoon, ten vehicles a company). The vehicle is airportable and armoured to give protection against small arms fire, shell fragments and flash burns. Protection against nuclear fall-out is also provided, and complete sealing and air-conditioning allows continuous occupation for four days. A heater or

Saracen with Swingfire Weapon System.

a refrigerator plant can also be carried to allow the vehicle to operate in arctic or tropical conditions. Other physical features include large side opening rear doors, torsion bar suspension, rubber shoe tracks for road running, a collapsible fabric flotation screen and associated nose buoyancy screen giving instant amphibious capability with propulsion (at four knots) from its tracks. The Rolls Royce multi-fuel engine is easily removable as a complete unit for maintenance or replacement. A large roof hatchway allows heavy weapons to be carried inside the vehicle. The commander's cupola mounts a GPMG or modified Bren and has a 360° traverse. The FV 432 was originally called the "Trojan" but this was dropped at an early stage as it conflicted with a registered trade name.

Brief details:
Weight 33,300 lb
Length 16 ft 9 in
Width 9 ft 3 in
Height 6 ft 2 in
Engine Rolls Royce K60 two-stroke C1
Speed 35 mph (road)
Range of action 360 miles

FV 432, Mk I
Initial production version, 54 built. This could not be used as a mortar carrier.

FV 432, Mk II
Main production type. Conversion of the basic vehicle to other roles is achieved by the addition of various kits which adapt the FV 432 to the following.

Armoured Personnel Carrier, FV432.

Carl Gustav
The platoon Carl Gustav anti-tank projector is mounted on a bar that is fitted across the roof hatchway of the standard vehicle.

81 mm Mortar Carrier
The mortar is mounted on a rigid base bolted to the floor of the vehicle and is sighted to fire through the main hatchway with a traverse of 360°. 160 rounds of mortar ammunition are carried and there is a crew of four.

Wombat
This role consists of mounting the Wombat infantry recoilless anti-tank gun to fire from the vehicle. The weapon is suspended in stirrups in the main roof hatch for this. The weapon can also be dismounted for ground

FV432 with Wombat.

FV432 with Carl Gustav anti-tank gun.

FV432 with 81 mm mortar.

81 mm mortar dismounted for ground role.

action, for which a light frame ramp is used. Fourteen rounds of ammunition are carried and there is a crew of four.

Command Post and Penthouse
Equipped as a mobile command post, the vehicle is fitted for some 40 different radio installations, mapboards and office equipment. It can be fitted with a collapsible penthouse which attaches to the rear of the vehicle.

Carrier Ambulance
In the ambulance role, four stretchers, two on either side of the vehicle, are carried on sliding swivel racks to ease loading and unloading. Alternatively two stretcher and five walking wounded can be carried.

Carrier, ARV

As an armoured recovery vehicle, the FV 432 is fitted with an eight ton winch mounted on a sub-frame fitted to the floor. An earth anchor is fitted on the hull rear. The winch is driven via the power take-off from the engine. Maximum pull of eight tons.

Bar-Mine Layer

The FV 432 is also used as a towing vehicle for the bar-mine laying equipment. Mines and operating personnel are carried in the vehicle and the equipment is operated from the open rear door of the FV 432.

Modified versions for other specific roles carry designation numbers as follows:

Carrier, Maintenance, FV 434

This version had been designed to carry major assemblies or replacement power packs for AFV casualties in the field. Stowed on the vehicle are special tools and equipment to deal with the replacement of damaged assemblies. The lifting device is a hydraulic operated Hiab crane specially adapted for the vehicle. A crew of four, driver, commander and two fitters is carried.

SP Mortar Locating Radar, FV 436

Developed for locating enemy mortar positions, this vehicle is similar to the basic vehicle, but has the rear of the hull cut away to provide a mounting for the Green Archer Mortar Locating Radar equipment. The crew consists of three men: driver, commander and radar operator.

Swingfire Launcher, FV 438

Modified as an anti-tank missile carrier, two launchers are provided on a fixed turret which has a periscopic sight. A 7.62 mm machine gun is mounted on a 360° rotating cupola.

Signal Vehicle, FV 439

This is a signals variant which can be equipped with various alternative sets of battlefield communication equipment, to adapt it for the roles of message centre,

FV 432 Command Post and Penthouse.

FV 432 as mine layer.

Carrier, Maintenance, FV 434.

Signal Vehicle, FV 439.

Right: *Swingfire Launcher, FV 438.*

Spartan APC. A new generation.

Spartan APC rear view.

telephone exchange, radio relay or cable layer. Externally various masts and cable reels are carried.

The FV 430 series has proved most successful and reliable in service. FV 432 APCs are most widely used by the infantry brigades of the British Rhine Army. While the unit cost of the FV 432 is relatively high (compared to contemporary foreign designs) this is generally considered acceptable in view of the excellent quality of the vehicle.

Spartan

This APC appeared in prototype form in 1971 as a member of the Scorpion CVR(T) family of lightweight air-portable fast AFVs. The Scorpion family as a whole was designed to meet combat conditions and requirements of the 1970s and the family of vehicles, all sharing a common chassis and automotive system, is designed so that various battlefield functions can be achieved. Of the series, Spartan was designed specifically to carry the five-man assault section of a Royal Armoured Corps tank squadron, their task being recce, demolition, obstacle clearing, or ambush work in support of the AFVs. Spartan, therefore, though carrying out a specialised type of infantry role is not an infantry vehicle and its function is quite distinct from contemporary APCs in British Army service. The vehicle has a driver, commander (with machine gun cupola), and seats for the assault section in a box-shaped hull. There is also stowage for weapons and demolition equipment. There is a rear access door and a No 14 radar set is an optional addition for battlefield reconnaissance work. Hatches in the hull roof allow the assault section to fire from the vehicle while on the move.

INDEX